INDIAN JOE BLOW

INDIAN JOE BLOW

*Pishikii-Kigeet-Black Eagle
Thunderbird Man.*

Chris Beach

authorHOUSE®

AuthorHouse™
1663 Liberty Drive
Bloomington, IN 47403
www.authorhouse.com
Phone: 1-800-839-8640

First published by AuthorHouse   07/26/2011

ISBN: 978-1-4634-2852-5 (sc)
ISBN: 978-1-4634-2853-2 (ebk)

Library of Congress Control Number: 2011911135

Printed in the United States of America

Any people depicted in stock imagery provided by Thinkstock are models, and such images are being used for illustrative purposes only.
Certain stock imagery © Thinkstock.

This book is printed on acid-free paper.

This Book is dedicated to the memory of my late son Joseph who ended his Short life March 25th, 2005 and also to all those who felt they had no other solution than taking their lives through suicide.

INTRODUCTION

Hi, I'm Chris Beach. With this book, I'm proud to present this play which deals with a very serious issue. More often than not, most first nation's people know someone very close to them who have tried to commit suicide and sometimes have been successful in killing themselves. Did You Know that 72% of our people have contemplated or attempted suicide? Our suicide rates are 500-600% greater than the national average. Those are not the only startling statistics with regards to our First Nations people. Contributions to these overwhelming facts are supported by such things such as:

- 64% of all children in care are First Nations
- Tuberculosis is 10 times higher in our communities
- 55% of First Nation homes in Manitoba either did not have adequate water supply/sewage disposal.
- Incarceration rates for our people are 9 times higher than non-First Nations.
- 1 in 3 female inmates are Aboriginal women
- Our people die on average 6 years sooner than other Manitobans.
- 40-50% patients at the Health Sciences Centre are First Nations people.
- Amputations due to diabetes are 16 times higher for our people than other Manitobans.

Chris Beach

Even former Prime Minister Paul Martin said back in 2004, and I quote;

> *"Aboriginal peoples have not fully shared in our nation's good fortune. While some progress has been made, the conditions in far too many Aboriginal communities can only be described as **shameful**."*
>
> PM Paul Martin—Feb 2, 2004

We cannot let another loved one take their life.

We cannot let another child grow up without their parents.

We cannot let our children believe that suicide is ever the answer.

We must do everything in our power to help each other.

Historically, our people depended on principles of character and virtue, of honour, honesty and respect.

As First Nations people, we had the ability to expand our knowledge and wisdom as a result of our connection to the Creator. Most of all we have great compassion for others, especially to those in need. A compassionate commitment, responsibility to all life, including our families, our friends, our children, and to the less fortunate.

We can achieve our vision and our goals by working in unity.

Cast of Characters

1. Joe

2. Black figure

3. White figure

4. Susan

5. Joseph

6. Paul

7. Mary

8. May

9. Tommy

10. Foster mom

11. Frank

12. Edna

13. Thomas

14. Mr. Matter

15. Prosecutor

16. Judge

17. Randy

18. Clerk

19. Frank

20. Doctor

21. Father Peters

22. Nancy

23. Narrator

Scene 1 Basement

Joe staggers down the basement stairs. He digs around in a desperate state. He reaches into a box and pulls out a dog leash and holds it high above him.

Joe (to the audience)

Yes, that's what I am, a stinken dog. No, I'm lower than a stinken dog. All my life, I've been treated like a stinken dog, kicked around and led on a short leash, making me beg. A dog probably gets more love and attention than I ever got. But today, I'm gonna show everyone what kind of stinken dog I really am. Screw the world and everyone in it. Pain and suffering is all the world has ever given me. I can't take it any longer, just can't stand it no more. I can't really explain this pain, or understand where it's coming from. It's like; I've been kicked in the stomach, hit with a baseball bat on the back of my head and stabbed with a large butcher knife, right through the center of my being. I wish someone would have just broken my bones, I could go see a doctor, he would cast me up or something, give me some pain killers and send me on my way. Sleep, oh how I long to sleep, the way I used to sleep when I was a kid. I haven't had a good night's sleep in such a long time. Oh, I would give anything for a good night's sleep, if it wasn't for this pain. Can't close my eyes without feeling this pain, and thinking of how messed up my life is, how messed up I am.

Two faceless figures start dancing around Joe, one dressed in black, that takes the shape of a man, one dressed in white, that takes the shape of a woman.

Black Figure (man's voice)

Go ahead, make them pay, make them suffer, make them feel what your feeling, make them hurt, the way they hurt you. Nobody loves you, nobody cares about, Ha, ha, ha, they're all laughing at you, ha, ha ha. Do it you fool, do it, You'll get the peace you've longed for, the never ending sleep.

White Figure (woman's voice)

No Joe, don't do this to yourself, don't listen to him, things will get better, things will be alright, please, I'm begging you, think about what you're doing. Leave this place, get out of the house right now, please get out.
Joe places his hands over his ears and tries to silence the voices. Still clutching the leash, he removes his hands from his ears and again searches around the room. He finds an old wooden chair and places it at the center of the room. He climbs up on top of it, and tries to find a spot on the floor joists above him to tie the lose end of the leash. He stops for a moment and looks towards the audience.

Joe (to the audience)

What? What the hell you staring at? You up there, thinking your high and mighty and then some, looking down on me. I know what you're thinking, but I'll tell you one thing, you have no right to judge me, you don't even know me. You don't know what I've been through. Think any of you care, another dumb Indian, no good to anyone, another welfare case, was only a burden to society, just another statistic. When you find me, you'll probably just shake your head, cut me down, and cart me away, like some road kill left abandoned on the side of the highway. Bet you in a week, you won't even remember my name, or that I was ever here, that I ever existed. You with your nice fancy houses, your nicely decorated perfect yards, your large suburban chunks of land, my ancestors were cheated out of, land we once roamed as a free nation. A place we would get arrested for even thinking of walking down your part of town. A place where you could close your blinds to the world, ignore people like me. You don't care,

6

we don't matter. A place where you could feel nice and cozy, safe from people like me and anyone who resembles me. Safe, what a laugh, you know, I once felt safe, yeah, that was a very long, time ago.

Joe jumps down from the chair and lays on the floor, curling himself into the fetal position. In the distance, you hear a drum beating and a soothing relaxing chant.

Joe (to the audience)

Hear that sound, that's the sound of my mother's heart beat. Listen to that beautiful sound. It's so nice here, so peaceful. Nothing to worry or care about, don't even have to think, just feel the warmth of my mother's womb, the soothing sound of her heart beating. I was once reminded of this sound, in a sweat lodge I went to. I was told by the elder that conducted it, that being in there, was like returning to my mother's womb, the womb of Mother Earth. The ribs of the lodge were like my mother's rib cage. The beat of the little boy water drum, was like my mother's heart beat. The water that was brought in there, was like the water that surrounded me in her womb. It was a place to leave all my inner garbage, a place where my grandfathers, grandmothers, the animals from the four directions, could take care of me. The turtle in the eastern doorway, the eagle in the southern doorway, the buffalo in the western doorway and the bear in the northern doorway. It was a place where I could get another chance, where my sins were forgiven by God our Creator, to be born again. A place, where I could once again, feel the safety of my mother's womb. I could begin my life all over again, take a good path, walk a good road, the red road, the sweet grass road. I felt so peaceful so safe.

Scene 2

In a small bedroom, Joe's mom and dad Susan and Joseph.

Susan

I just came from the nursing station, the doctor said I'm going to have a baby. I can't imagine a baby growing inside me. You're going to be a father. The doctor said my due date is March 17th. I'm so excited; we're going to have a baby.

Joseph

What do you mean; we're going to have a baby? I can't be a father, I'm only 15 years old, I have plans, things I want to do, places I want to see. I've got no time to be a father to no one. I don't want to get stuck in this God forsaken reservation. There's nothing here, this can't be happening.

Susan

What do you mean? I thought you said you loved me? I thought you'd be happy. I thought a baby would bring us closer together, you know, something made from the both of us. A baby is a gift from God, to love and care for.

Joseph

Where did you get that idea from? Babies just tie you down, they cry all the time, never shut up. They stop you from living, screw up your life, just like the way they screwed up my mom and dad's life.

Susan

Well, you'd better get used to it, when this baby comes of me in March, you won't be able to push it back in. This baby's growing inside of me and you're going to be a father, whether you like it or not.

Joseph

No way man, you tricked me, just to trap me into marrying you or something. You never asked me, if I wanted to be a father.

Susan

Well excuse me, you should have thought about that before you got into my pants. What did you think was going to happen, all those times we had sex together.

Joseph

Well, I don't like it one bit, and, if I knew you were going to pull stupid and and have a bastard kid, I never would have slept with you. Anyway, you don't have to keep it, you could get rid of it, if you really loved me, you would get an abortion.

Susan

You mean, kill my baby? I can't believe you would ask me to do such a thing. Kill my baby, our baby. You don't get it, do you? This is your flesh and blood, your child, our child.

Joseph

Hey, it's not even human yet, right now, it's just a tiny piece of meat, anyway, it's probably not even mine.

9

Susan

What you talking about Joseph? Of course it's yours, I ain't been with anyone else but you, and you know that.

Joseph

Yeah, right, I seen the way you look at my friends, when they come over to visit me. Maybe one of them is the real father, and you're just a slut, trying to snag me down.

Susan starts to cry.

Susan

I can't believe you're talking to me like that, you said, I was your only love, that we would be together, forever, that you would take care of me, I believed you.

Joseph

Well, that was before you pulled stupid, and went and got yourself pregnant. I told you, I don't want to have a stupid kid, and I'm warning you to get rid of it, or else.

Susan

Or else what?

Joseph

Or else, you'll never see me again, and that's one promise, I will keep.

Joe (to the audience)

No, no, no, I want to live, don't reject me, I'm your son, your own flesh and blood. I'll be good, I won't give you any trouble, I promise, I won't cry.

Joe gets up off the floor and faces the audience.

Joe (to the audience)

Yeah, I was rejected, even before I was born.

Scene 3

A woman and a man sitting on a living room couch. (Susan's mom and dad, Paul and Mary). The television is loud, a hockey game is on, the reception is snowy, and the picture starts rolling.

Paul

Damn, can't even watch a stupid game on this piece of junk.

Paul gets up and starts hitting the side of the television set. Mary seems timid and afraid.

Mary

You want me to get you another beer honey? You want a sandwich or something?

Paul tries to adjust the television set, he's ignoring Mary. Susan walks into the living room, also looking timid and scared

Susan

Mom, dad, I have to talk to you.

Paul is still fixed on the television set, Mary hands him a beer.

Susan

Mom, dad, we need to talk.

Paul

I'm listening, and so is your mother.

Susan

No you're not, you never listen to me.

Susan starts to cry. Paul turns off the television and he and Mary both face Susan.

Paul

This better be good, I'm missing a really good game right now.

Susan

Mom, dad, I went to see the doctor today, at the nursing station.

Mary

Are you alright?

Paul

And?

Susan

I don't know how to tell you this? I'm pregnant; I'm going to have a baby.

Paul and Mary become silent for a few seconds.

Paul

What? What the hell you talking about? Your only 14 years old for crying out loud. Who did this to you? I'll kill him.

Susan

No dad, I love him.

Paul

What do you mean you love him? You don't even know what the hell love is. Your just a kid, you don't know anything, your just a baby having a baby.

Paul gulps his beer down.

Paul

Well, you're not going to keep it; I don't want any bastards around here.

I don't need another snot nose kid disrupting my life. You're going to get rid of it, you're going to have an abortion.

Susan

No dad, I want my baby, I'm going to keep it.

Paul

What? You don't talk back to me, I'm your father and you will do as you're told. I didn't raise you to become a little slut, just like your mother. One bitch in this house is enough.

Susan

Mom, say something.

Mary bites her lip and doesn't say a word, she has a real distant look in her eyes.

Susan

But dad.

Paul

No buts about it, you're getting rid of that damn kid and I don't want to hear another word, you hear me?

Susan

No, I won't, I keeping it.

Paul

Why you little whore, I'll teach you to talk back to me.

Paul gives Susan a backhand across the face. He knocks her to the floor and kicks her in the stomach. Mary jumps in front of Susan in an attempt shield her, Mary screams.

Mary

No, don't hurt my baby.

Paul again raises his hand in an attempt to also give Mary a backhand.
He stops himself.

Paul

Awe, Damn it.

Paul grabs his beer and storms out of the room.

Joe (to the audience)

See, I told you, rejected, and not even in the world yet. I've been told, my mother packed her bags and hitched a ride to the big city of Winnipeg.
Some say Winnipeg's a dangerous place to live in. Sometimes, it's the murder capital of Canada. But, I guess, she thought it was a safer place for me and her. She had the address of her aunt May, from an envelope she took from her mother. It was in Winnipeg's north end, a rooming house on Flora Ave.

Scene 4   Rooming house

Susan knocks on the door. It opens and a large drunk woman answers.

Susan

Excuse me, does May Flett live here?

May

Yeah, I'm May, and who in the hell are you?

Susan

I'm Susan, Susan Thickfoot, My mother is Mary, your sister, you are my auntie.

May

Oh wa, the last time I saw you, you were still in diapers. So, how's your mother doing? I haven't seen her in a dog's age.

Susan

She's doing ok, I guess.

May

Well, you might as well come in, make yourself at home.

May leads Susan into an old, run down, one room apartment.

It only has a bed, an old table, and a couch.

May

Sit down; do you want to have a beer?

Susan

No thanks, I don't drink.

May cracks open a beer.

May

So, how's that ass hole of a man, my little sister married?

Susan

You mean my dad?

May

Yeah, what a jerk, I told her to leave him years ago, treats her like some kind of an animal. I don't know what she sees in him anyway, never worked a day in his life, I guess some woman can't live without a man. No sir, not like me, no man will ever boss me around. I do ok by myself, but your mom's another story. So what brings you to the big city?

Susan

My dad kicked me out, I mean, I ran away.

May

What you go and do that for?

Susan begins to cry.

Susan

I'm pregnant, my dad won't let me keep my baby, and he wants me to get rid of it. I don't want my baby to die.

May

What about the father, where's he in the picture?

Susan

He doesn't want the baby either.

May

Awe, men, forget them, they're all losers anyway, especially your dad. You know, he came on to me one time, he wanted to do me. I said, you're crazy, your my baby sister's man, he said he didn't care. He tried to force himself on me, I broke a beer bottle over his head, cut him pretty bad. He told your mom, I tried to come on to him, the bastard; she's never talked to me since. Men, all they want from you is sex. Are you sure you don't to have a beer?

Susan

No thanks.

May

You know, since I was a little girl, I think the whole reservation wanted to do me. I was 4 or 5 at the time, when they started on me. They would come over to my place, when my mom and dad were drinking. At first, they would just fondle me on their lap. Then, when I got a little older, they would wait until my parents were passed out. Then, they would make me go all the way, you know, make me do things to them, them do things to me. I couldn't do nothing about it then, but, I'd like to see any man try and do me now, use me like a dirty dog again. Come on, have a beer with your old auntie.

Susan

I don't like beer, it makes me sick.

May

You know, I almost killed a man once, he tried to do me, when I was passed out. Yeah, went to Portage for a while, you know, the jail for women. Even a couple of women tried to do it to me in there, I let the bitches have it. Yup, from now on, nobody does me, unless I give them my permission. So, where you gonna live? Where you staying?

Susan

I don't know, I was hoping I could stay here with you.

May

What? In this shit hole of a place, barely enough room for me, let alone, you and a baby.

Susan

Well, just for a little while, till I can find something else.

May

Well, you can stay as long as you like, it's not much, but what the hell, family has to take care of each other. Are you sure you don't want a drink? Sure helps me when I'm feeling down.

Susan

Well, maybe, ok, I'll just have one; I guess one can't hurt, but only one.

Joe (to the audience)

You know, I heard my mother never stopped drinking from that day on. At first, she drank lightly, till she became a heavy drinker. Her favourite drink was wine. Everyone told her, she was going to have a wine-o baby, and she would laugh. I don't think she knew what the alcohol was doing to me, while I was in her womb. I was born February the 10th, a little over a month before her due date. I weighed a whopping 3 pounds 11 ounces. I almost didn't survive, but somehow I pulled through. No one came to see me or my mother, in the hospital, except my mother's aunt May.

Scene 5   Hospital room

May

He's a beautiful baby boy.

Susan

Yeah, he looks just like his dad; I wish he was here to watch his son come into the world.

May

Like I said honey, men, all they want is one thing, sex, can't depend on them. You know, they're not going to let you keep him.

Susan

Who won't let me keep him? Who you talking about?

May

You know, Child and Family Services, they're baby snatchers.

Susan

Why? What business is it of theirs anyway?

May

They always take our babies from us, I hear they take them and ship them all over the place. People say, they even get a good buck for them, from rich families in the United States, families who can't have children of their own.

Susan

You're a liar; tell me that's not the truth.

May

Sorry, but I ain't no liar, that's the honest to God truth.

Susan

No ones gonna take my baby and sell him.

May

Hey, I must have had over a dozen children, all of them gone, I don't even know where they are. Child and Family Services took them all, one by one.
I never saw them again.

Susan

Never, can they do that?

May

Afraid so, they got the power. We are just baby making machines to them.

Susan

Don't you miss them?

May

Forgetting herself, almost in tears.

Of course I miss them, that's probably why I drink so much, just to forget all that shit and stuff. I hear they're somewhere in the United States, sold to the highest bidder. They treat our babies like animals, just like cattle being herded to the slaughter house, and we got no say, none at all.

Susan

My babies not a cow, I won't let them take my baby from me, they can't.

Joe (to the audience)

From that day on, my mother's aunt May gave me the nickname Pishikii, the ojibway word meaning cow. Maybe it's because, she said I was going to be treated like one, sold just like cattle. Or, maybe it's because of the way I looked, when she first saw me. I was labelled with a condition called, Fetal Alcohol Syndrome. A Doctor in Winnipeg diagnosed me. I had a face that kind of looked like a cow's. My eyes were further apart, my nose was kind of flat and I had no upper lip. Aunt May joked, I was lucky I wasn't born a girl, I'd have no place to put my lipstick. Even in school, other kids would tease me and call me a cow. I didn't think it was funny, and besides, a cow is a girl, me, I'm a boy. They say in the Indian culture, children have no gender. Yeah, once I asked one of my foster moms what Fetal Alcohol Syndrome was. She told me, it meant, that I was retarded, that I would never amount to anything, I was damaged goods. Yeah, that's what I am, Pishikii, a retarded cow.

Aunt May was right, not long after I was born, Child and Family Services took me from my mother. I really don't remember, yet, somehow, I think it really affected me. I found myself having overwhelming feelings of loneliness, that I was in this deep, large empty void, I would never climb out of. I would sometimes dream my mother would be standing at my door, coming to take me home, but it never happened. I was placed in over 7 different foster homes, each time my foster parents would find some excuse to get rid of me. I was in lots of houses, but I never had a real home, a real family. Everything seemed as fake, as the cold and uncaring smiles of my many social workers, always telling me, this was all for my own good. Nobody ever gave me nothing that didn't have strings attached. Like the time my social worker told me, I was supposed to get new clothes. As it turned out, my new clothes were my foster brothers hand me downs. My foster mother used my clothing allowance to buy him new clothes. Although, I did manage to get a nice Nike hoody, my foster brother couldn't fit no more. It wasn't new, but it was a Nike. One day my foster brother wanted it back, and my foster mother made me give it to him. He just laughed. I was about 8 years old at the time, I think he was 14. One night I got up to use the washroom. It was really late and I had to walk past my foster brother's bedroom. I heard strange noises coming from inside. His door was slightly opened, so I walked in on him. He had his hand on his penis and he was stroking it. His name was Tommy.

Scene 6   Bedroom

Joe

Hey Tommy, what you doing?

Tommy jumped from his bed and pulled his blanket over himself.

Tommy

What the hell you doing in here? You got no right coming into my bedroom without knocking.

Joe

I heard noises; I thought you were sick or something.

Tommy

Well, you should knock before you come into someone's bedroom.
Don't you Indians have doors, or do you still live in tepees?

Joe

So, what were you doing?

Tommy

None of your damn business, and if you tell anybody, I'll beat the shit right out of you, you hear?

Joe

I won't tell anyone, I promise.

Tommy

Well, you better not or I'll tell everyone, you're nothing but a dumb Indian liar, who always tries to steal my stuff.

Joe

But, I never stole nothing from you.

Tommy

I don't care. Hey Joe, since you're here anyway, why don't you sleep in my bed tonight? Come on, come and lay down with me.

Joe

Are you sure? Your mom might get mad.

Tommy

Don't worry, she's asleep, she'll never find out, come on, lay with me.

Joe

Ok, I'll lay with you for a little while.

Joe crawled into Tommy's bed.

Tommy

Hey Joe, You want that Nike hoody back? I know you really like it.

Joe

For real, can I?

Tommy

Yeah, of course, but there's something I want you to do for me.

Joe

Sure, I'll do anything for that hoody.

Tommy

Come, bring your hand and touch me here.

Tommy moved Joe's hand to his penis.

Joe

No way man, I don't want to do this, that's gross, anyway, I'm a boy, not a girl.

Tommy

Come on, you said you'd do anything for that hoody.

Joe

Yeah, but not that.

Tommy

You want me to call my mom, and tell her you came in here to steal.

Joe

But I never . . .

Tommy

Who do you think my mom's gonna believe? Me, or a lying retarded Indian like you. Now bring your hand, not like that you dumb Indian, like this. Oh yea, that feels good, yea, like that, now open your mouth.

Joe

No way man, no way.

Tommy

Not so loud you dink, you'll wake up my mother.

Tommy grabbed Joes head.

Joe

(Coughing and spitting)

What you do that for you bastard?

Tommy

I told you to be quiet, if my mom finds out, she'll send you away.

Joe

I don't want to sleep with you no more; I'm going to my room now.

Tommy

No you're not, I'm not finished with you yet.

Joe (to the audience)

Tommy grabbed one of his socks and folded it into a ball. He shoved it into my mouth, turned me over and used me like a woman. I never felt so much pain in all my life. I couldn't yell or scream. I think my spirit left my body and traveled somewhere else. I just lay there like I was dead; I think I was in shock. You know, this went on for a few months. Tommy came into my bedroom almost every night. He even started calling me, his little Indian bitch. One night, his mother accidently walked in, and caught us together. She had a look of shock in her face. She walked to my bed and grabbed me by my hair. She then smashed my face against the wall, my nose started bleeding.

Scene 7   Joe's bedroom

Foster Mom

Tommy, get to your room fight now. Don't you ever let me catch you in hear again.

Tommy grabbed his clothes and left the room, his mother also left and came back with a long black thick belt. She had a look of rage in her eyes.

Foster Mom

You little bastard heathen, nobody else wanted you, and out of the goodness of my heart, I take you in, and this is how you repay me. This is the thanks I get. You try and turn my son into a bloody faggot.

Joe

It wasn't me . . .

Foster Mom

My Tommy's a good boy, you're the evil one. I was warned not to trust good for nothing Indians like you, devil worshippers. You're a whore, just like your mom.

Joe

No, you don't even know my mom, and I never did nothing, Tommy made me do it.

Foster Mom

Lies, all lies, to top it off, you tell lies. My Tommy would never do such a thing.It was that devil in you that made him do it. But, I gonna fix you, I'm gonna beat the devil right out of you. Make sure you never do this to anyone else.

Joe (to the audience)

She beat be until I blacked out. I remember waking up the next morning in a whole lot of pain. She called my teacher and told her I was sick and wouldn't be in school for a while. She said she would kill me, if I said anything. I never did say anything, mostly because I felt so much shame, and really did believed it was all my fault. I should never have gone into Tommy's bedroom that night. If I would have minded my own business, none of that would have happened.

A few weeks later, my worker showed up and I was moved to another foster home. It was on a farm, a married couple named Frank and Edna. They had two boys, a little older than I was. At first, It seem like it was a good placed to be, I thought this was gonna be my last move. Everyone had to get up at 6 am to do farm chores. We had breakfast and me and my two foster brothers went to school. I was allowed to eat in my room, I don't know if they didn't want me eating with them, anyway, I didn't mind, cause I didn't like nobody watching me eat.

We would run to the main road to catch the school bus to go to school . . . I always sat at the back and believed I was well hidden. Sometimes, I would pretend I was part of the bus itself, that I blended into the vinyl yellow seats. In the classroom I did the same thing, sat as far back as I could. I wanted to be left alone, not bother anybody, not have anybody bother me. My teacher was a very scary big white woman. I was afraid of her and never wanted to get on her bad side. She would let her wicked old glasses fall in front of her face and give you a mean condescending stare. I wore my hoody up all the time and pulled my hands into my sleeves. You know, the hoddy Tommy gave me. I'm not really sure why I kept it, maybe it's
because it was the only thing I felt belonged to me. I sat there like a piece of furniture, with no connection to anyone or anything. I never made eye contact, always had my head down. I think I was afraid that if people looked into my eyes, they would find out stuff about me. I didn't want anybody knowing anything me, especially what Tommy used to do to me. I guess when you've been abused like I was, you just shut yourself down, I wouldn't let nobody in, I couldn't trust nobody. My room was in the attic, it wasn't finished, but at least it was my own space. It was often cold and draftee, but no colder than the world I was living in. We went to church every Sunday and would have to sit through a long boring service. Father Peters, as they called him, would always talk about sin and going to hell. One Sunday, he even

talked about aboriginal people doing their witchcraft, and how God was punishing them by making their world a bad place to be in, not to mention, that they were going straight to hell. One day it occurred to me, that if I went to heaven and my people weren't there, why would I want to be there. I longed to be with my own people, and if hell is where they are at, I guess that's where I also want to be too. Yeah, me Indian Joe has decided, I'm hell bound anyway, so why fight it. Late one Sunday evening, I was lying in bed unable to sleep. I guess Frank and Edna thought, I was already sleeping, and I couldn't hear them. They were talking about me.

Scene 8   Frank and Edna's bedroom

Edna

You know, the family fair is in two weeks.

Frank

So, what about it?

Edna

Well, I didn't want to say anything, but this has been bothering me for a long time.

Frank

What are you talking about?

Edna

What are we going to do about Joe?

Frank

Take him with us of course.

Edna

We can't take him with us, what are people going to say?

Frank

I'm still not sure what you're talking about.

Edna

Well, Joe has dark skin, we have white skin, and people will stare at us, you know, him being Indian and all.

Frank

So, what's wrong with having an Indian boy with us? We're doing our Christian duty you know.

Edna

I know, but people might think, that Joe is my child, that I had an affair or something, that I slept with some drunken Indian, kind of like the ones you see hanging around the bars in Winnipeg, bumming for money to buy rubbing alcohol and stuff.

Frank

Well, we just can't leave him here.

Edna

I can just imagine the looks I'm going to get, people whispering behind my back. It's going to drive me crazy.

Frank

Well, you and the boys go for the weekend. I'll stay here with Joe, we can spend the time catching up on some farm work.

Joe (to the audience)

Well, I guess this Indian wasn't going anywhere. I was feeling very angry and rejected. I can't help it if my skin colour was darker than theirs. That's the way God made me. I began to hate my brown skin and God for making me different. After that night, I even began hating Edna. I thought she was such a nice person, that she cared about me. Now I know the truth, can't be seen with me, what a witch, evil to the bone. I couldn't help but to think of why Edna took me in, in the first place. Then it occurred to me, maybe she was doing it just for the money. I was special needs, because I had Fetal Alcohol Syndrome. Child and Family Services were paying her big bucks. Frank, talking about doing his Christian Duty. I was an extra hand to do the farm work. A slave that who does what he's told. I wonder how much Christian duty he would be doing, if he had to support me from his own pocket? Is that what Jesus did when he walked on Mother Earth? Say to people, for $29.95, I can save your soul, I don't think so. He's probably looking down on them thinking, are you people crazy? Yeah, while I was in the system, I began to realize, that I was just, extra income, non taxable funds, a cheap labour slave, a cheque every two weeks. Edna and her two real sons left for the fair early Saturday morning. They were all dressed up and seemed very excited. I told myself, I didn't want to go anyway, but deep down inside, I was hoping Edna would change her mind. I had never been to a fair in my life. I heard, they had rides, races, where you could win some money, eat lots of great food, like hot dogs and cotton candy. I even heard, that natives from neighbouring reserves and villages would also be there. It would be nice to see people with the same colour skin as I have. Maybe even play with some of their children, maybe even find or meet some of my relatives. All those thoughts quickly faded, as I watched Edna and her two real sons get into their car, drive down the main road and disappear out of sight.

Frank and I spent the day doing odd jobs around the farm. We then went into the house. Before Frank started making supper, he went into the cellar and brought up a 24 case of beer and two bottles of whiskey. I didn't even know he drank at the time. I always saw him as a church going Christian man. It didn't take him long to get drunk, and it was like he became a different person. He started talking and looking at me in a strange kind of way. It was like, another side of him began to surface. When the food was ready, I asked Frank if I could take my food to my room, as I always did. He insisted, I eat supper with him at the table. I began feeling very uncomfortable around him, and I felt like running away.

Scene 9   Kitchen

Frank

I'm a very good cook you know. I used to cook all the time, before I met Edna.

I put my head down and said nothing.

35

Frank

Why do you always wear that stupid hoody, and pull your sleeves over your hands? Even on a hot day, you wear that damn thing.

I began getting even more uncomfortable and started pulling my sleeves even more tighter over my hands.

Frank

Hey kid, do you want to have a beer?

I shook my head from side to side.

Joe

No thanks.

Frank

What? An Indian that doesn't drink, I don't believe it. When I was in Winnipeg, I never met an Indian that never refused a bottle. In fact, they would do just about anything for the price of a six pack, if you know what I mean. Come on, have a beer, I know you want one.

Joe

No thanks, I don't want one.

Frank

Do you think you're too good to have a beer with me? Don't insult me, take this beer and drink with me, this time, I'm not asking.

Frank shoved that beer in front of me, grabbed my face with his other hand and squeezed both side of my cheeks until he opened his mouth. He then poured the beer down my throat, gave me my first taste of alcohol. It was kind of bitter, I then took the beer from Frank and drank it all down. I didn't want any trouble with Frank, so I continued drinking with him.

Frank

Yeah, I knew you would like it.

I think I was on his third or fourth beer, when Frank started to move closer to me.

Frank

Let's see what you look like under that hoody of yours, most of you Indian kids are very good looking when you're young, have very smooth and soft brown skin. It's when you get older; you get all fat and ugly.

Frank tried to pull my hood down. His hand started shaking and he began breathing a little heavier. I pushed his hand away and tried to stand up.

Joe

No, leave me alone, please, let me go to my room now.

Frank was a big strong man; I couldn't resist him when he grabbed me by my shoulders and pushed me down into my chair.

Frank

You have nothing to be afraid of, as long as you do as I ask, just sit still and don't give me any trouble.

I became afraid of Frank by then and let him pull my hood down. Frank began running his fingers through my hair.

Frank

You know, you Indian kids have very nice thick dark black hair, so soft, and it smells so nice too.

Frank put his face on my head and began smelling my hair, breathing heavy at the same time. He put his arms around me and tried kissing me. I tried to move my head away, but Frank grabbed me and tried to put his tongue his mouth. He rubbed my chest and slowly moved his hands towards my privates. The memory of Tommy doing this to me started to enter his mind. I jumped up and pushed Frank away yelling.

Joe

No! I don't want this to happen, not again.

Frank

You mean you've done this before. So what's the problem? You think you're too good for me, or something. You know, you and I could become real good friends, I could make life real easy for you, you just have to do something for me.

Joe

No! I don't want to do this, please don't make me do this, I'll tell your wife.

Frank

Why you little Indian bastard, you think anyone's going to believe you?

Joe (to the audience)

Frank grabbed me by the hair and dragged me into his bedroom. He slapped me around for a while and then threw me on his bed. I begged him to stop, but he went into a rage. He did me in my mouth, then ripped off my clothes and started pumping me like a woman, kissing me with his tongue in my mouth. I could taste his beer shit breath and smell his unwashed body odour, all over me. He turned me over and used me like a woman. I screamed, cried, and yelled from the pain, pleading with him to stop, but my screams seemed to bring him more pleasure. He was like some evil sadistic animal, getting his jollies by inflecting pain on me. I lay there helplessly, trying to block out what was happening to me. But, there was no one to rescue me, no one to hear my cries for help, no one to get this lunatic pig off of me. We were all alone, my screams were unheard by him, God, and the rest of the world.

After he was done, he held me close to him and went to sleep. I lay there very still, afraid to move. I didn't want to wake him up, for him to continue attacking me. When he started snoring, I knew he was fast asleep. I lay there a little longer and then slipped my body from under his arm. I quietly moved around the bedroom to find my torn clothes, and went to dress in the dining room. I remember becoming very angry and ashamed. My whole body was aching and my shoulders were bruised from his large hands clutching me as he gratified himself. I went into a panic and then a rage that engulfed every inch of my body. I think that may have been the very first time a really thought about killing myself. I was so fed up and disgusted with what Frank had done to me and at that moment I believed suicide was going to be my only way I would be able to get away. I looked around the room and found some left over line that Edna had used to make a clothes line outside. I picked up the line and decided to head out to the barn to hang myself. On my way out the door I then noticed my foster brother's baseball bat he had left by the front door as he came inside for supper the day before. Another idea then entered my mind and I decided, there and then, this bastard wasn't going to hurt me again. No ones gonna hurt me anymore. I threw the line across the room and picked up the baseball bat and crept slowly back into Frank and Edna's bedroom. I lifted it high into the air. I think I saw him wake momentarily, as one of his eyes began to open. That's when I started hitting him on the head, then, on every inch of his wretched body. I'm not sure how many times I hit him, but I do remember smacking that desirous smirk on his face. He and I were both covered in blood. I thought for sure I had killed him. I found his wallet and took a total of $86.00 before throwing it back into his face. I pulled my Nike hoody off, threw it against the wall and kicked it on my way out. I then changed my clothes, packed my bags and hitched a ride to Winnipeg. I spent the next two weeks living on the streets, sleeping in back lanes, and park benches. I wasn't alone for long, because there was a lot of other people living on the streets, most of them were young people like me, running from one thing or another. One night, I was sitting at a bus stop and a boy a few years older than me, started talking to me.

Scene 10 Bus Stop

Thomas

Hey man, you got a smoke I can bum off you?

Joe

Sorry, but I don't smoke.

Thomas

Hey man, that's ok, my name's Thomas, what's yours?

Joe

Why, are you a cop or something?

Thomas

Are you kidding? I hate cops, nothing but a bunch of pigs. A few times they picked me up, just so they can beat on me. I think they get their jollies from beating on Indians.

Joe

Cops are supposed to help people, not beat them up. You know, like on that TV show I used to watch, I think it's called, I don't know, something about the law anyway.

Thomas

Are you kidding, that's just TV and stuff? Cops aren't really like that. Sure when they're on TV and the camera is on, they act nice and all, but in real life, they're just a bunch of pricks. See this scar on my left eyebrow, got that from one of those long flashlights they carry. They sometimes even shoot and kill Indians, and get away with it too. Like a friend of mine, I think he was 17 years old, Cops said he was a suspect in a robbery. My friend ran and they shot and killed him. They said, why did he run? He didn't want to get beat up of course.

Joe

Didn't you tell anybody? They can't just go around beating up people.

Thomas

Sure they can, they got the power. Who you gonna tell anyway? Nobody's gonna listen to you, especially if your an Indian. Another friend of mine told me, that some cops picked him up and dropped him off somewhere on the outskirts of the city. It was a very cold night and wet snow was coming down hard.

Joe

What did he do?

Thomas

He was lucky, a slow moving train happened to come by, and he hitched a ride on it. He said he almost froze trying to hold on. Anyway, he made it back alright, barely though.

Joe

Why didn't you tell your parents? You know, your mom and dad.

Thomas

Parents, that's a laugh, I got no parents. I was in foster care all my life, moved around from one foster home to another. Child and Family Services, were my mom and dad. I was nobody's child, a cheque every two weeks, that's what I was.

Joe

Yeah, I know the feeling.

Thomas

You know, they said they were gonna help me, when I was old enough to get my own place. They called it, independent living. They did get me a place, but that didn't last very long. One day my welfare worker told me, that I was young and should find a job. I tried to find a job, but most people look at you as some Indian in a gang, or a thief that can't be trusted. No one would give me a job, my worker stopped my cheques, and my landlord kicked me out, for not paying the rent. Those welfare workers treat you like shit, like it was their own money, coming from their own pockets. If us Indians stopped getting into trouble with the law, if our kids stopped being taken by the system, Think of how many jobs would be lost. How many Judges, Lawyers, police, guards and social workers wouldn't have work. We would probably wreck the whole effen economy. If it wasn't for people like us, they wouldn't even have a job.

Joe

Yeah, that's really messed up. How long ago was that?

43

Thomas

Over two years ago. You know, I hear people say, that we have life easy, us Indians, living off the government and all, getting everything for free, just because we have a treaty card, we never pay taxes, we're living on the gravy train. They should try and live my life, then come and tell me how easy I have it.

Joe

Wow, I've only been living on the streets for about two weeks now, don't know if I could do it for two years.

Thomas

It's not that bad in the summer time, you can sleep just about anywhere. It gets real tough in the winter time, you know, trying to keep warm and all. I sometimes find an exhaust vent, from a building. It blows warm air out. Sometimes, I even sleep on them, till I get chased away.

Joe

I was in foster care too, didn't like it, so I left.

Thomas

Are you in any trouble?

Joe

No, I just decided to run away.

Thomas

You know, most of us street kids are from foster care. I read somewhere, that 90% of street kids, are from foster care. They take you from your real families, and put you in homes that only want you there for the money. Then, when you turn 18, you're on your own. The family you could have had are not there anymore, yeah, no one to turn too, no one to even care.

Joe

That really sucks.

Thomas

Yeah, they don't care about us, so I do what I gotta do to survive. Hey, you got any money?

Joe

No, I spent my last few bucks on a couple slices of pizza. That was two days ago, I haven't eaten since. What do you do for money for something to eat? What do you do when you have to eat?

Thomas

Sometimes I go to the soup kitchens, or, I work the street.

Joe

What do you mean, you work the street?

Thomas

You know, I stand under a bridge, downtown, and some old guy picks me up, and we go somewhere dark. I give him, you know, what he wants, for 10 or 20 bucks.

Joe

Are you gay?

Thomas

Of course not, I just hate doing it. But, sometimes I get so cold and hungry. Sometimes, I even get lucky and get taken to a hotel room. They feed me, and I have a warm place to stay for the night. Hey, sometimes I make a little more, if I let him go all the way with me. But, I make sure, they use a condom. Don't want to get aids and stuff.

Joe

Wow, I don't think I could do something like that.

Thomas

Hey, when you get desperate enough, you'll do anything. It's hard at first, but after a while, you get the hang of it. Sometimes, those old guys are really fat and ugly and they make you want to puke, but, it puts coin in your pocket. Hey do you want to give it a shot? Make some money, to buy something to eat.

Joe

I really don't know if I can.

Thomas

Come on, you're young and nice looking, not like you got anything else to do to make some cold hard cash.

Joe (to the audience)

Thomas took me under his wing and showed me how to survive on the streets. I became a male prostitute and was doing things to anyone with cash. It was tough at first, but after a while, I kinda numbed my emotions with street drugs. I didn't take me long to get hooked on them and I found myself turning more tricks, just for the drugs. I often didn't even think about food and would go for days without eating. At one point, I was turning so many tricks, that on the street I was given the name, "Indian Joe Blow". I really didn't care if I lived or died, me and my life were all screwed up. Once in a while I would bump into Thomas and we would hang out together. He was a really great guy and he became the only real friend I had. One night, Thomas and I were smoking crack under the bridge, when he started talking crazy. He said, he was really getting sick of how his life had turned out. He didn't want to do it anymore and he was planning to go somewhere far away. I really didn't understand what he was talking about, and I asked him what he meant. He said he really didn't know where, anyplace but here. I told him he was talking crazy and I wanted him to stop. He then laughed and we started talking about other stuff. For some strange reason, he seemed very different. I never knew him to be so happy. It was a bit unusual, considering the life him and me were living. It was as if he had just gotten a load off his chest and didn't have a care in this world. We both fell asleep, and when I woke up early the next day, I found him hanging from under the bridge. I was in total shock. He looked all pale a blue, with his belt wrapped around his neck. He was just hanging there, like and old rag doll. I never knew anybody that committed suicide before, and it really messed me up big time. I found out later, that this kind of thing was very common in a lot of aboriginal communities. In some places, the suicide rate was 4 to 7 times the national average. I heard it was a real epidemic, that nobody really wanted to deal with. Sure they try some sugar coated cheap programs that really don't get to the root of the problem, and I'm not sure why. Maybe it's because the Christian community always said, suicide was a one way ticket to hell, or maybe people think that if you even mention the word, you'd be promoting it. Just ignore it, and maybe someday, like magic, it will all go away or something. I just can't imagine, that someone like Thomas, could end up in a place like hell. I tried not to think about it, because it just made me more confused and angry about God. Anyway, someone decided to call the cops and they came and cut him down. They asked me some questions, and it was then I realized, that I didn't even know his last name. I'm not sure what they did with him, where they took his body and all, I never went to his funeral or ever found out where he was buried. I would have liked to visit his grave site, but I never knew where it was. I never talked about him to anyone, but the memory of me seeing him hanging there, always haunted me. Although I felt very abandoned by him, I will remember Thomas, as a true friend, someone I would miss and never really get over. Not long after that, I got arrested for offering an undercover cop a job for $20.00. At first, I gave him a fake name, as I always do, but he slapped me around until I gave him my real name. He ran my name in his computer and found out I had a warrant for my arrest, for beating Frank to near death. I always thought I had killed Frank, I wasn't sure how to feel about finding out he was still alive. I really had mixed feelings about that. Anyway, they charged me and I was sent to the Manitoba Youth Centre. In a way it was a good thing, even though my freedom was taken away, because it gave me a chance to get off the street drugs and get cleaned up. I don't think I would have lasted much longer living on the streets, doing what I was doing. A few months later I found myself in court charged with theft under and aggravated assault. Because I was a minor, I was tried, as a young offender. You know, you learn a lot about yourself in a courtroom, things you don't know, and things you don't want to know. My lawyer was a young white man, by the name of Mr. Matter. He was a legal aid lawyer, a government appointed hand me down. He only came to see me a couple of times, before my court date, I really didn't tell him anything, I think he believed, I did it for the money. I was too ashamed to tell him the truth. Besides, who they gonna believe, a dumb retarded Indian like me, or a so called big church going man like Frank. Of course they made him look like some saint or something, a victim of circumstance.

Scene 11 Courtroom

Joe's thoughts are heard as he walks around the courtroom. No one else hears or sees him, except the audience.

Mr. Matter

Your honour, Joe was apprehended by Child and Family Services at a very young age. At the time, they felt that his mother, Susan Thickfoot, could not care for him, because she herself was only 15 years of age. She was an alcoholic and was also addicted to various street drugs, such as crack cocaine. She resorted to street prostitution to support her addiction. As a result, Joe was born with a condition called Fetal Alcohol Syndrome. He does not have the cognitive ability to fully understand the consequences of his actions. He was born with a smaller than average brain and has the mental ability of a 8 year old child. His judgement is continually impaired and will often will react in a compulsive nature. He has never been able to socialize with his peers and is illiterate. Throughout his life, he was placed in a number of foster homes because of his difficulty controlling his behaviour. In short, he suffers from a severe form of mental retardation.

Joe

See, even my lawyer thinks I'm retarded.

Mr. Matter

Joe's mother made a few attempts to try and get Joe back, she even went to a couple of different treatment centres, to try and kick her addictions, but without success. She died from a drug overdose, when Joe was 5 years old.

Joe

What? My mother's dead, and no one ever said anything to me. What the hell is wrong with you people? Keeping something like that from me. Oh my God, I just can't believe it, my mother's dead, mothers don't die, they can't.

Mr. Matter

Your honour, I don't believe Joe, should be held responsible for the crimes he has committed, because I don't believe he fully understands what he has done. I beg you to consider all the factors that contributed to Joe's delinquent behaviour.

Joe

Frank sat there with his wife and two sons throughout the whole trial. All the while I felt like screaming. Hey, what about me, I'm the real victim here, not him. You don't know what that bastard did to me. Once in a while I would look his way, wanting to beat the crap right out of him all over again. Come on you low life piece of shit, try and use my body like an old dead dog again, just try, next time, I'll make sure you're dead.

Prosecutor

Your Honour, Frank is a hard working devoted father. He attends church every Sunday, and is a God fearing Christian man.

Joe

God fearing my ass, he got me drunk and raped me, don't make me laugh, if you only knew.

Prosecutor

He and his wife Edna, opened up their home to this ungrateful young man. They gave him everything he needed, a stable home, plenty of love, and a safe place to live.

Joe

Safe, what do you know about safe? You weren't there, nobody's safe, around this low life. And love, they don't know the first thing about love.

Prosecutor

And, what did they get in return? Frank hasn't been able to work his farm ever since that terrible day; and all for what, few measly dollars? In fact, he was beaten so bad, my client has no memory of that day at all, because of the injuries inflicted on him by this savage young man.

Joe

Yeah, how convenient, he can't remember, you mean, he doesn't want to remember. Tell him Frank, tell the judge what you did to me, you pig, he's the savage, not me.

Prosecutor

Your honour, you need to set an example of these hoodlums, so that upstanding citizens like Frank and Edna won't continue to be victimized. Lock him up, in a place where he can't do anyone else any harm.

Joe

Frank's the one who should be locked up, I'm not the bad guy here, he is.

Prosecutor

I beg you, your honour, please, give Frank and his family the justice they deserve.

Joe (to the audience)

Justice, what is justice? I've heard the word a lot in my lifetime, but never really understood its meaning. Once, Thomas looked it up for me, in a dictionary, and told me it meant, the determination of rights according to the rules of law or equity. Whose laws, whose rights? Don't I, Indian Joe
Blow, have rights too? Yeah, justice seems to be a word only used by others, to justify their own selfish actions. When the first Europeans came here, did they want justice for everyone? Or, did they only say the word when it would benefit them? Did they

even consider the people who where here first? My ancestors, the people who welcomed them and showed how to survive, who wanted to share Mother Earth with them. They then later come with a piece of paper saying that the land my people had lived on for thousands of years, was owned by someone else. That my people had to disappear and go away. Just because some big government official, signed his name on the dotted line. That Mother Earth could be something you could own, something you didn't have to respect, something you could exploit, rape and ravish, make her waters undrinkable. Devastate the land, so there's nothing left for our children, and our grandchildren. And when we refused to vacate the land, they kill all the buffalo, trying to starve us to death, inflict us with diseases, deadly to our people. Lock us away on reservations, junk land that nobody else wanted, hoping we just die off. Burn down our Sundance Lodges, in order to ram Christianity down our throats. Tear us from the arms of our mothers and fathers, and put us in residential schools, to teach us how to become good white people. Cut off our hair, the source of our strength. Not allow us to communicate, by forbidding us to speak our language. And when, they were finished raping and beating our spirits into the ground, they ship our children all over the world, like cattle, in hopes we wouldn't return. For those who managed to survive and fight back, they built large prisons to lock them away forever. Tell us, we're bad people, who don't deserve to have rights. Teach our youth, not to have hope, or any kind of future. As a result, we've become slaves to a world of addiction and prostitution, drug dealing, as a means of coping and surviving. All in the name of, justice, whose justice?

Joe is now seen standing in front of the judge, slouched with his head down.

Judge

In my courtroom young man, you will stand up straight and tall, and look me in the eye.

53

Joe straightens out and looks at the judge.

Judge

You've done a malicious thing to this family, and now, I have to decide what kind of punishment you deserve. The crimes you have been charged with are very serious, and it seems to me that money was your only motive. Do you have anything to say, before I pass judgement on you?

Joe

No, nothing.

Judge

Do you have any remorse for what you have done?

Joe (to the audience)

I really didn't know what the word remorse meant, I looked at my lawyer and then to the judge. I was afraid to ask and didn't really what to say, so I just turned to the Judge and said, No.

Judge

What kind of an animal are you? You beat a man almost to death, you rob him, devastate his wife and children, and you have no remorse.

The judge then shook his head.

Judge

If I could, I would put you away for the rest of your life. But, because of your age and the Young Offenders Act, I can only send you away until your 18th birthday. Take him away; get him out of my sight.

Joe (to the audience)

I spent the next three years of my life, in a boy's institution, about an hour's drive from Winnipeg. When I turned 18, I was given my clothes and a bus ticket, back to the big city. When I arrived in Winnipeg, I remember feeling a sense of freedom, but also a sense of being very lost and all alone. I didn't know anybody and wasn't sure what I was going to do next. I took a room at the Salvation Army, while I tried to figure out what to do with my life. I noticed a lot of native people living there, and some of them, looked, in pretty rough shape. Some even reminded me of army veterans, who had just returned from some kind of catastrophic war. Some were missing limbs and in wheel chairs, their faces beaten and badly scarred, with a nose so punched in, that it lay almost flat to one side of their face. Watching them, come in and out of their realities, brought me an overwhelming sense of hopelessness and despair. They were on a road that went nowhere, in a dark tunnel, with no light to guide them. For the first time, I understood what it meant, when people would call them, the walking dead. They were my people, once strong and mighty, reduced to a living of shame and desolation. They seemed to drag their feet on the ground as they walked, with their shoulders slouched, and heads hung low. Stripped of every ounce of dignity and pride, like this place was their last stop in life, a dead end road, with the only exit being death. Once on a street corner, I watched a small group of them gather. They were drinking a bottle of something, probably rubbing alcohol, and passing it around. They were, having a conversation, and once in a while, someone would say something, and they would all laugh. I felt like going up to them and saying, what's wrong with you people? Look at you, there's nothing funny about the way you are living, you got nothing to laugh about. I kept my distance from most of them, because, they were a constant reminder of the way I was feeling, way down deep inside. I kept telling myself, that somehow, someway, I had to find a way out of here. I felt, if I stayed, I'd end up like one of them. Like, if I got too close, some of what they had, would somehow rub off on to me, and I'd one day wake up to this continual nightmare. I did manage to make a friend with one of them, a young native guy named Randy.

Scene 12 Salvation Army lobby

Randy

Hey man, what's your name? Where you from?

Joe

My names Joe, but I'm not really sure where I'm from.

Randy

That sucks, me, I'm from a reserve about a two hour drive north of Winnipeg, down the # 6 highway. My parents moved here when I was 6 years old. Things were ok at first, until my parents started drinking heavy. Well, to make a long story short, I was apprehended by the System, you know, Child and Family Services, I stayed in a few foster homes until I turned 18. Then, the cheques ran out, and I had no place to go, so I ended up here. What's your story?

Joe

What do you mean?

Randy

I mean, how did you end up here, in this place?

Joe

Oh, I was in foster care too, all my life, I don't remember my mom and dad, I was too young. I found out my mother died, but I'm not sure where my father is.

Randy

Do you know his name, here he's from?

Joe

I was told by one social worker, that his name is Joseph Threefingers, but that's all I know. I sure would like to hook up with him someday.

Randy

Know what? I'm pretty sure I've heard that name before. There was a man who used to come and party with my mom and dad. I'm sure that was his name. It's not a common name, and a name you don't forget.

Joe

You know where he is now?

Randy

I'm not exactly sure, but, I think he's the same man I've seen going into a hotel on Main Street a few months ago, maybe he lives there.

Joe

You think so?

Randy

Could be, If you want, I'll take you there tomorrow.

Joe

Really, you know, I've always dreamed of having a real father, maybe things will be ok now, when I find him.

Joe (to the audience)

The next day, Randy and me walked down to the hotel. It wasn't far from where we stayed, and as we walked, I imagined, I would meet a tall native man with long black hair, maybe braided on both sides. Something like, Chief Dan George, a proud and funny man. He would call me son, and I would call him dad, and we would hug each other. Maybe he's a medicine man, who smokes a ceremonial pipe and smudges with sweet grass. Someone who maybe, Sundance's and runs a sweat lodge outside the city.

Someone people have respect for and look up too. Like those elders that were invited to the institution, I spent the last three years in. Soon, I would have a father, a family, a connection, and a purpose in life. Just like some of the stories that were read to us, when we were kids in school. We would go for walks in the park, maybe ride the bus together, go to a movie, hey, even go to the zoo. When I was a kid, I would dream, my real father would come to my foster home and say son, I'm taking you home now. He would take me for a burger and fries and tell me everything would be ok. I would go for rides on his shoulders and he would carry me home. Our home, a real home, where I wasn't just a cheque every two weeks. Yeah, a place where I would be happy and safe, just my father and me. It was already late in the afternoon when we got to the hotel. I stared at the building for a while, not sure if I wanted to go in. The place looked very dingy and run down, and I began to wonder, why my father would stay in such a place. I kept thinking that Randy, had taken me to the wrong place, that there must have been some mistake.

Scene 13 Hotel

Randy

Hey Joe, are you just going to stand there? Or, are you gonna come in?

Joe

Randy, are you sure this is the place?

Randy

This is the place alright, come on, let's go see if he's here, let's go find him.

Joe and Randy walked into the lobby and went to talk to the clerk behind the desk, he was smelly and unshaven.

Clerk

Hey, can I help you boys?

Randy

Yeah, is there a man living here by the name of Joseph Threefingers?

Clerk

Who wants to know?

Randy

Well, my name is Randy, and this is my friend Joe, his dad is Joseph
Threefingers. Does he live here?

Joe

No, I don't think he lives here; we must be in the wrong place.

Clerk

Hey, Joseph never talked about having a son.

Randy

So, you do know who he is?

Clerk

As a matter a fact I do, he lives here alright, you'll find him upstairs in room 311. But no visitors past 11 o'clock, you hear.

Randy

Don't worry; we'll be gone by then.

Joe

Look Randy, I really don't think this guy is my dad, maybe we shouldn't go up there.

Randy

Come on, it's gotta be him, how many people do you think have the name, Joseph Threefingers.

Joe

Still, I don't think it's him.

Randy

Well, there's only one way to find out, come on.

Joe (to the audience)

We went to the stairs and climbed to the third floor. The hallways seemed dark and gloomy. I began feeling very uneasy as we came closer to room 311. When we got there, Randy knocked on the door, but no one answered. The door was slightly opened, so Randy decided to push it open all the way. He stuck his head in and waved for me to follow. We walked into a dingy run down suite, with nothing but a small table, a dresser, a small black and white television set, propped on an old wooden chair, and a single bed with and old man sleeping in it. The place was filthy with old wine bottles and Lysol cans littering the floor. I stared at the old man for a little while. His pants looked wet from pissing himself and the whole room smelt of urine. His clothes were filthy, his hair was messy and greasy, his face unshaven and dirty.

Scene 14 Hotel suite

Joe

Come on let's go, that's not my father, it can't be, my father's a medicine man or something. There's no way this low life is my father.

Randy

Wait, I'll wake him up.

Joe

No, leave him, that's not my father.

Randy went to the bed and shook the old man.

Randy

Hey wake up, Joseph, wake up.

The old man opened his eyes, rubbed them and jumped up.

Joseph

Who in the hell are you? Who let you in here? You don't get out right now, I'll call the cops.

Randy

Well, we knocked, and when you didn't answer, we noticed the door was opened, so we walked in.

Joseph

Well, you can just get the hell out, just as fast as you came in. Got anything to drink.

Randy

No, sorry.

Joseph

So get out then.

Randy

Wait, are you Joseph Threefingers?

Joseph

Yeah, so, what's it to you?

Randy

Did you once have a girlfriend named Susan Thickfoot?

Joseph

Yeah, she run off and left me, I thought I'd never see her again. I came to Winnipeg to try and get her back, but, she wouldn't come. She kept saying, the only reason I wanted her back was to do her, don't know where she got that idea from. You know, sometimes you say or do things without thinking, you mess them up so bad, that nobody trusts you no more. I guess that's what I did with Susan, no matter what I said, she just wouldn't believe me. She died a few years later, I never did get over her, you know, I really did love her.

Joe (to the audience)

My heart started pounding as the old man started answering Randy's questions. I prayed he would answer no to all of them. My heart sank every time he answered yes. I wanted to run and hide somewhere, but my feet felt like they were stuck to the floor. Inside I kept screaming, no, no, this just can't be my father. My father is a young man in his early thirties, this guy looks like he's in his seventies. There's gotta be some mistake, but each time I looked at him, I began to see myself. I had some of his facial features, his body structure. He kinda looked like me, but a hundred years older. I tried to convince myself, it wasn't him, but, Randy kept asking him questions, and he would answer them, as only my father could.

Randy

Well, did you know Susan had a son, your son?

Joseph

Yeah, that's what I heard, a boy named Joe, I never got to see him, Child and Family Services took him away, I guess he'd be about 18 by now. Do you know him? You know where he is? I've always wondered about him, always wanted to see him.

Randy

Well, he's standing right in front of you. Joseph, meet your son Joe, Joe meet your dad Joseph. I told you it was him.

Joseph

Joe, Joe, my long lost son Joe, is it really you? Come give your old man a hug.

Joe (to the audience)

Although I always wanted to find my father, but, this is not what I expected, I moved towards him and gave him a hug, at the same time wishing we hadn't come here. This frail shell of a man was my father. What happened to him? What made him this way? My image of my father was shattered that day, and I was totally devastated. I never felt so much anger, so much shame.

Joseph reached under his bed and pulled out a bottle of wine.

Joseph

Come here my son, come and have a drink with me. Hey you guys got any money for another bottle?

Randy

Here, I only got a couple of bucks, take it.

Joseph

What about you Joe, got any money, for your old man?

Joe

No, I got nothing.

Joseph

What about a smoke, you guys got a smoke? I haven't had a smoke since yesterday. I have some old butts that I went and found on the street, but
I got no rolling paper, no tobacco.

Joe (to the audience)

Tobacco is one of the four sacred medicines. It was given to us by God our Creator for us to us to smoke during communication. To use in our Ceremonies and offer up in thanks giving. To give freely to our elders for their knowledge. It was something we always used to give, before we took. Allowed us to have a relationship with and have respect for all living things; to acknowledge and honour our grandfathers with. Today, it's been stripped of its sacredness, by the modern day world. It's been exploited and turned into a billion dollar industry. In exchange, we are reduced, like my father, to a cigarette butt picking man. Picking butts off the street, like some starving dog begging for scraps. And when we try and sell it ourselves, we are arrested and thrown in jail. While some rich people, sitting high in their big mansions, look down on us poor butt picking selves.

I told my father, I needed to use the washroom. I went into this cockroach ridden place called a bathroom. A place to get cleaned up in, but it made me feel more filthy than when I went in. I rubbed the mirror with my sleeve, to clean it, and then took a long hard look at myself. At the same time, I began to realize, I really didn't know who I was, who this person was, staring back at me. What am I? Why am I here? All I could see was my father looking back at me. Is that my fate? To become an old man before my time, a drinking butt picking bum, with no purpose in life, but to wait, just wait for death to relieve me of my torment. I grabbed my head, dropped to my knees and whined like the helpless dog, that I felt I was. I never went back to that hotel room, to see my father again. I guess I was too disappointed, too hurt. It was too painful, to see the man, who is responsible for me being on this earth, to be living in such a lowly state. I just wanted to forget him, pretend I was never there, believe my father was someone else. Sometimes, when someone would ask me, about my father, I would make something up. I would even go as far as saying, my father was dead. Even when I found out that he really died, about a year later, from alcohol poisoning, I never went to his funeral. I don't think anyone went, or if anyone cared. Once I thought, that I should at least visit his gravesite, but for some reason, I never did. The father I wanted to remember, was the father I created in my mind, many years ago when I was a small child. Only my friend Randy knew the truth, but, he never said anything.

Randy found a job at a roofing company on the outskirts of town. The starting wage was $9.00 an hour. He said he would talk to his boss, to see if he could get me a job there too. His boss told him to bring me in the following Monday, and he would try me out. I was a nervous wreck the whole weekend long, thinking about starting a new job. I would be making a lot of money, maybe I would be able to finally buy some new clothes, maybe even save enough to buy myself a good used car. I rode the transit bus with Randy, early Monday morning. He gave me an old pair of work boots and I was all set. His boss said I was a hard worker and he hired me on full time. The work was dirty and backbreaking, but I was happy to have a job, and I couldn't wait for my first paycheque. For the first time, I felt good about myself and I was in control of my life. I even rented an apartment in the north end of Winnipeg, and it was great having my own place. One Friday night, after a hard day's work, Randy and I went to a bar to have a couple of beers. We sat there for a few hours, just talking and laughing, when I noticed a pretty Native girl looking at me. She was wearing tight blue jeans and a very revealing blue shirt. She wore glasses and had very long blue-black shiny hair. At first, I was too shy to go and talk to her, but after a few more beers, I managed to gain enough courage to walk over and say something. She was with another girl.

Scene 15 bar Room

Joe

Can I buy you girls a drink?

Both girls looked at each other and laughed.

Fran

Go ahead, it's a free country.

The both laughed again.

Fran

My name is Fran, and I think you are kind of cute, why don't you come and
 sit with me, and my friend Gwen?

Joe

My name is Joe, and I would love to come and sit with you girls, but I'm here with a friend of mine.

Fran

Well, tell him to come and sit with us too, the more the merrier.

Joe

Hey Randy, these girls want us to come and sit with them, you want to join them?

Randy grabbed the beers and moved to their table and sat down.

Fran

Well, aren't you gonna introduce us to your friend?

Joe

Oh, yeah, Randy, this is Fran and her friend Gwen, and girls, this is my best friend Randy. Fran, that name is different.

Fran

It's short for Francine, but I prefer people call me Fran.

Joe

Oh, ok, Fran it is.

The four of them stayed at that bar until it closed at 1:30 a.m.

Joe

Hey, Fran, what you gonna do after we leave this place?

Fran

I'll probably go home, unless you have something better for me to do.

Joe

You want to come and chill at my place for awhile?

Fran

Where do you live?

Joe

On Burrows Avenue . . .

Fran

I don't know, you got any beer?

Joe

No, but I can get some.

Fran

Alright, as long as you promise to pay my cab home later.

Joe

You got yourself a deal.

Joe (to the audience)

Randy and Gwen hopped in one cab and Fran and I went in another cab. We took the cab to my place. I was kind of nervous being alone with Fran. She was the first girl I was ever interested in and I wasn't sure if I could even have sex with a woman. In the past I was only with men, not by choice, but by circumstance. I wasn't sure about my sexuality and guess I really believed I was gay, although I never enjoyed being with men. But, laying beside Fran, made me feel so good, she smelled so nice, and her long black hair against my face, just gave me the shivers. I could feel my body shake, every time I put my arms around her. She started kissing me and I just melted in her arms. As we lay on the couch, Fran started to undress me, and I started undressing her. I was very nervous and excited at the same time. We had sex a few times that night, and that's when I realized, that maybe I wasn't gay after all. Most of all, for the first time, I was in love, with someone who loved me. As it turned out, Fran had a part time job at a chicken restaurant. It wasn't long after, she moved in with me and we became a couple. I was real happy living with Fran and for a while life couldn't have been better. She came home one day, all in a glow.

Scene 16 Apartment

Fran

I have something important to tell you.

Joe

Yeah, I love you too.

Fran

No, I'm serious, listen.

Joe

Okay, I'm listening.

Fran

I went to the walk in clinic, after work today. You know, I missed my time and I've been feeling sick lately.

Joe

And, are you okay?

Fran

Well, the doctor did some tests, and he told me that I am pregnant.

Joe

You're what?

Fran

I'm pregnant, are you mad? Don't be mad.

Joe

What do you mean?

Fran

You're going to be a father.

Joe

Wow, why should I be mad, I'm going to be a father, I'm so excited? All my life I've always dreamed of having a family, and now, I'm really going to have one. Maybe you better sit down, don't do anything.

Fran

I said I was going to have a baby, I didn't say I had a rare disease.

Joe

You know, everything seems to be so different.

Fran

What do you mean?

Joe

Well, once I had nothing, now I have my own place, I have a job, I'm in love and now, I'm going to be a father. My life is so perfect now.

Joe (to the audience)

Fran quit her job when she was on her eighth month and went on employment insurance. I tried to spend as much time as I could with her, fussing over her and the baby all the time. Every payday, we would go shopping, to buy something special for the baby. I was like a kid on Christmas Eve, waiting for Santa to come. One night she woke up to tell me her water broke, and it was time to have the baby. We called a cab, and went straight to the hospital. She was rushed to the delivery room, and I stayed with her the whole time.

Scene 17 Delivery Room

Doctor

Okay, Fran it's time to push, yeah, that's right push.

Fran

Aaa, aaa, it hurts aaa, Joe help me, it hurts, aaa.

Joe

It's okay Fran, I'll hold your hand, I'm here, and I'm not going anywhere.

Doctor

I'll give you an epidural, it will help with the pain, you can relax for a while.

Joe

What's that you're giving her?

Doctor

It's a needle, I insert in the lower back, to help with the pain. Okay, Fran a little longer and it will be all over, now push.

Fran

Aaa, aaa, aaa, oh my God, aaa

Joe (to the audience)

After about two hours, Fran gave birth to our little baby girl. At first, all I saw was a little opening, about the size of a quarter. I could see was the top of the baby's head. The opening got bigger, with each push Fran made. Then all of a sudden the baby just popped out. I was so amazed, it was a real miracle.

Joe

Fran, Fran, oh my God Fran, it's a baby girl.

Joe (to the audience)

The doctor started cleaning up our daughter, and she let me cut the Umbilical cord, it felt as if I was cutting a garden hose. A nurse then came in and took her to another room, to further clean her up.

Fran

Joe, follow her, don't let her out of your sight.

Joe (to the audience)

I followed my baby and the nurse to the next room and watched the nurse as she cleaned my daughter. I'm not sure what happened next. The nurse went into a panic and started calling for the doctor. My baby started turning blue and the doctor and another nurse came running in. The second nurse took me outside and asked me to wait in the waiting room. I didn't want to go, but she insisted. A little while later the doctor came, and told me my daughter was born with a heart condition, and didn't make it, that my baby died of heart failure. I could hear Fran yelling and screaming in the background. My whole body went cold and numb. You know, things were never the same between Fran and I. It seemed like we became strangers, like we no longer knew each other. It was very hard for me to show any emotion during this time. I think a large part of me died, with my little baby girl. We had a small funeral service at a funeral home on Main Street. A few of Fran's family and friends showed up, along with my best friend Randy. I was really glad Randy showed up, because I really didn't know what to say or do, to help Fran. She seemed so cold and distant. It was as if, someone crawled into her body and sucked out every bit of life, she had. She couldn't hug me and I couldn't hug her. It's not that I didn't want to hug her, I guess we really didn't know how, to react to each other. We never talked about losing our daughter, I thought, that if we didn't talk about it, it wouldn't hurt so much, and the pain would all go away, then, maybe things will get back to normal. We named her Angel, because she was our little angel. She looked so pretty, in her little pink dress, as if she was just asleep, and would soon wake up. I wanted to pick her up and hold her, in my arms, and tell her how much I loved her. I wished I could say to her, wake up my little girl, come see daddy. She never did wake up, and neither did Fran. I had a hard time looking at Fran, maybe it's because I knew she was in so much pain, and I didn't know how to deal with it. Randy was a big help, because he was there for Fran, when I couldn't be. Every time Fran and me would make eye contact, she would start crying uncontrollably. After the funeral, Fran and I went back to our apartment, It seemed so cold and empty. I think we both stopped living for a while. For some reason, we even stopped having sex altogether. Every time I would ask her for sex, she would turn me down. It was kind of strange, the more she rejected me, the more I wanted to have sex with her. Anyway, I had to go out of town for a couple of weeks, we had a big roofing job to do in another city. Fran didn't seem to mind, In fact, she seemed happy about me leaving. We finished the job a couple of days early, and I thought I would surprise Fran, by bringing her some flowers. Maybe later, I would take her out to a nice restaurant, for a meal. It was about 2:00 in the afternoon, when I arrived home to my apartment. At first, I thought Fran wasn't home, when I walked into the living room. Then, I heard a noise in the bedroom and I walked right in. What I saw next, shocked the hell right out of me. There was Fran, in bed with another man.

Scene 18 bedroom

Joe

Fran. What the hell are you doing? How could you?

Joe (to the audience)

I felt like killing someone, my mind went blank, I reached over and grabbed the guy and threw him against the wall. I was shocked even more when I saw who it was.

Joe

Randy. Randy, what the hell are you doing? Of all the people in the world, I never would have believed you would do such a thing, oh my God, I think I'm gonna puke.

Randy

Sorry man, you know how it is.

Joe

Yeah right you, you bastard; friends don't do that to each other.

Joe was so mad; he punched Randy in the face. Fran started yelling.

Fran

Leave him you ass. It's over, me and you; you can get the hell out. I don't love you anymore, I love Randy. Anyway, what are you doing here? You're not suppose to be home . . .

Joe

The hell with you, how could you? In our place, in our bed. What the hell's wrong with you?

Joe points his finger at Randy.

Joe

You get the hell out of my place, right now, before I kill you.

Fran

You got no business to tell anyone to get out, you get the hell out.

Joe

This is my place, I pay the rent, work my ass off, and what thanks do I get, you bring my so called best friend home, and do him in my bed.

Fran

Well, Randy was there for me when Angel died. I told you to watch her, but you didn't, you just let her die.

Joe

What the hell are you talking about, it's not my fault

Fran

Yeah right, you didn't even care, you never cried, not even once, when we lost our little baby girl.

Joe

What are you talking about? Of course I cared, you have no idea how much I cared. You think, because I held it all in, trying to be the strong one, that I didn't care. I saw how much pain you were in, I didn't want to burden you with my own pain. Oh my God, how could you even think, I didn't care about losing Angel?

Fran

Yeah right, the only one that was there for me was Randy, Randy took care of me, made me feel better, he loves me, you don't, you never did.

Joe

You think I would have put up with you all this time, if I didn't love you. All those times you were rejecting me, and I still stayed. Meanwhile, you were messing around with my so called, best friend.

Joe turned to Randy.

Joe

I thought I told you, to get out.

Fran

No Joe, I want you to get out, I told you, I don't love you anymore, and it's over, you get out.

Joe (to the audience)

I'm not sure what happened next, I think I lost it and walked out. They can have each other, I didn't want to stay with someone who doesn't love me. I started drinking heavy to try and forget Fran and Randy. My boss fired me for coming to work drunk one day. Everything I had, everything I worked so hard to get, was all gone. Lost forever, and once again I was all alone. And it was all her fault, her and my so called best friend, what a fool I was. I had no one to turn to, nobody I could trust, my life was all messed up, just like before. I found myself on the streets again, doing drugs and drinking anything I could get my hands on. I ran out of money and I started working the streets again. Indian Joe Blow was back in action, do anything to anybody, for a price. I didn't care anymore; I had nobody to care about me, not even myself. One night, when I was working the streets, a car pulled up with an old man in it, he stopped and picked me up. I got into his car, and we drove off.

Old Man

Hey, son, how much do you charge, for you know?

Joe

Forty dollars, and if you want anything else, it will cost you more.

Old Man

I tell you what, I'll give you thirty dollars, and not a penny more.

Joe

Hey, don't I know you from somewhere?

Old Man

No, never saw you before in my life.

Joe

Father Peters, is that you? I can't believe it's you. I always thought of you as real holy man. You once told me, I wasn't pure enough, and here you are trying to have sex with me, for money.

Father Peters

You must be mistaken, I'm not Father Peters.

Joe

Don't lie, I remember you, you were the one that told me my people would end up in hell for practicing their culture, you told me they were nothing but devil worshippers, doing witchcraft in their Sundance's and sweat lodges. You're the reason, I was ashamed of who I was, the reason I couldn't embrace my own culture, worship God the way my ancestors did. And now, you're here, asking me how much I charge to do you.

Father Peters

I told you, you must have me confused with someone else.

Joe

Liar, I will never forget how you used to make me feel, every Sunday, Condemning my Elders, and putting my people down, talking about the devil and sin. I wonder what the devil thinks of you now?

Father Peters

Listen, I don't know what you are talking about, I'm not who you think I am.

Joe

Damn rights you're not. You stood up there, on your pedestal, acting like you were some saint from God. Telling people how bad they were, making them feel like shit. Did you tell them you go around picking up young guys for sex?

Father Peters

I'm sorry; I don't know what you mean?

Joe

You don't get it do you? And you were the same one, passing out a petition for the people to sign, because you were against same sex marriages. Causing people to hate one another, because they happen to have a belief that was different from yours. Now you want to have sex with someone of the same sex. Do I look like a woman to you?

The car stopped.

Father Peters

I've had just about enough of you young man, get the hell out of my car, right now.

Joe

I hate you and all you stand for, you lying bastard, you ain't no father of mine.

Father Peters

I said, get out, right now.

Joe (to the audience)

I opened his door and jumped out, and as he drove away, I kicked his car. I was so turned off by him and his hypocrisy, I felt like killing someone. Was anyone in this stinken world real? Or, were they all pretending to be something or someone else. Was everything they were supposed to stand for, just another stinken lie? Just a mask they were wearing to cover up their real selves; showing phoney smiles with fake intentions. The more I thought about it, the more insane I felt. It sickened me. Was there anybody I could actually trust? When I really thought about it, the more confusing it became. I really tried to shut it all out, with all the drinking and drugs I was doing, but it got to a point, where they didn't seem to be working anymore. The world, and all its bull crap, was just too much for me to handle. I just couldn't take it anymore. So one night, I went to a house party and decided I was going to have a good time, for the last time. That's where I met Fran's cousin Nancy.

Scene 19 Party house

Nancy

Hey, Joe, how are you doing?

Joe

I'm okay, I guess.

Nancy

What do you mean, I guess? Either you are, or you're not.

Joe

I don't know, I just feel like shit right now.

Nancy

Why you look so down Joe? Things can't be that bad, come on cheer up.

Joe

Well, you know, I guess you heard about what happened between me and Fran?

Nancy

Yeah, I knew she was a bitch; hey forget about her, you'll find someone else, someone better, you'll see.

Joe

Well, it's not only that, you know, it's a bunch of stuff.

Nancy

Like what?

Joe

I don't know, just stuff.

Nancy

Well, I'm sure you'll get over it, just don't think about it, it will depress you too much, try and have some fun.

Joe

I just can't take it anymore, nothing ever works out for me, I just feel so shitty.

Nancy

Nothing that a little beer and a few pills can't fix, I'm sure.

Joe

I'm just so tired of it all, like I want it to be all over.

Nancy holding a bottle of beer in one hand and some pills in another.

Nancy

Well, after a few more of these, and a few more of those, nothing will seem as bad as you think. By morning, you'll be just fine, always works for me.

Joe

Well, I just feel like ending it all.

Nancy

What you talking about Joe?

Joe

You know, kill myself, I got nothing to live for, no reason to stick around, I just feel, I just want to die.

Nancy

Awe, come on Joe, don't talk like that, you shouldn't say those things.

Joe

But it's true, I am really thinking about doing myself in.

Nancy

Life can't be that bad.

Joe

If you only knew, but it really doesn't matter anymore anyway, soon it will be all over.

Nancy

Listen Joe, you're talking crazy; I want you to stop talking like that.

Joe

Like what, everything I'm saying is true, I've been thinking about it for a long time.

Nancy

Thinking about what?

Joe

Weren't you listening? Do I have to spell it out for you, I'm going to kill myself.

Nancy

No you're not; you're just saying that, I know you're only joking.

Joe

It's no joke.

Nancy

Come on Joe, now you're really scaring me, stop talking like that right now, promise me, you won't talk like that no more.

Joe

Okay, I won't talk about it anymore.

Nancy

You promise.

Joe

I said I would, didn't I?

Nancy

Here have a beer, try and have a good time, that's what life's all about, having a good time.

Joe

Yeah, I guess you're right.

Nancy

I know I'm right, don't talk about it, and it can't happen, it's as easy as that.

Joe (to the audience)

I waited until everyone had passed out. It was there and then, I decided I was going to do it. I was in a whole lot of pain. I think my spirit had already left my body, because I felt like I was floating in the air, looking down on myself. I looked around the room and found the door to the basement. I opened the door and slowly crept down the stairs. Now here I am, just me and all my pain, and all of you guys watching me.

The white and black spirits start moving around Joe again.

Black Spirit (man's voice)

Come on, in a few minutes, all your pain will be gone forever, do it, ha, ha, ha, no more lies, no more suffering, just a deep, deep sleep. It won't take long, do it, do it you fool, do it.

White Spirit (woman's voice)

No Joe, don't do it, don't destroy yourself, don't listen to him, you're a young man, you've got a lot to live for, leave this place now, get out, get out, get out of this house, now, please Joe get out, before it's too late.

The two spirits continue to dance around Joe.

Joe (to the audience)

You know, I bet many of you have travelled all over the place, to get to know other people, learn about other cultures. It's too bad, you didn't take the time to get to know me, learn a little about my culture. I'm someone practically from your own back yard, maybe you wouldn't have feared me.

Too bad, you didn't take the time to sit and talk with me, instead of always trying to pass judgement on me. I would have really liked for you to have listened to me, with a caring and understanding ear. Sure, I've done some bad things in life, but overall, I'm not such a bad person, am I? Who knows? Maybe you and I could even have become friends. And maybe, just maybe, it would have made a difference, for me and so many others like me. So the next time you see me, on some street corner, give me a smile and I will try and smile back. But most of all, I'm begging you to at least acknowledge me, as a human being, one of God's creations, as one of your many brothers, whom you shared Mother Earth with. I wonder if anyone will miss me? I wonder if anyone even cares. I wonder if anyone will even show up for my funeral? I doubt it. All I ever wanted was to be loved. Is that too much to ask for? Wasn't that Jesus' last commandment; to love one another? Isn't love one of our 7 teachings? Yeah, I'm talking to you too. Does anyone love me? Been made to feel that even God doesn't love me, and now, I don't even love me.

Joe points to people in parts of the audience.

Joe (to the audience)

Hey, you down there, do you love me? Hey, you over there, do you love me? Hey, you over there, do you love me? Hey, what about you up there, do you love me?

Joe then climbs back up onto the chair, the dog's leash still wrapped around his neck. He then grabs the loose end of the leash and ties it up above him, and then kicks the chair from under him.

KIGEET PART TWO

Cast of Characters

1. JOE

2. POLICE MAN

3. GRANDMOTHER

4. GRANDFATHER

5. THOMAS

6. SUSAN

7. JOSEPH

8. Blue Thunderbird Woman

9. ENERGY

10. Narrator

11. Black Figure

SCENE—1

Scene begins with JOE hanging from a dogs leash in a basement. He is there for a couple minutes before his spirit leaves his body and starts to walk around; He looks at himself in bewilderment, staring curiously at his lifeless body. He then tries to touch his body but his hand seems to go through it. He doesn't realize the guy hanging there, is in fact himself.

Joe

Hey you wake up, who are you? Why you hanging there like some dead dog. Talk to me, are you listening to me? I said talk to me. Do you need some help? Do you want me to call somebody? Hey, I'm only trying to help, don't ignore me. Say something. Ok, let's try again, do you need some help? You know, if you don't want me to help, just say so and I'll go away. You'll never see me again, I promise, I'll go away and that's the last time you'll see of me. I can take a hint, I'm used to being ignored, not listened too, it's been like that all my life, people pretending I'm not there, like I never existed or something, like I was just a sack of potatoes, just sitting there taking up space. Awe, come on please, and just talk to me, say something. Hey, you know what? You don't look so good. I think you might have some sort of problem. You're so still and quiet, like your dead or something. You Know, I had a friend who looked like you, all pale and blue, I forget why he looked like that. He think he went and done something to himself. When I tried to touch him, he seemed so stiff, so cold. I tried calling his name, but he wouldn't respond, he just kept hanging there. His name was, you know what? I forget his name. I remember running around screaming and crying for someone to help him, but no one would. They just walked on by, like they didn't see him or something. I even went up to one guy, and grabbed him by his arm and pleaded with him to help my friend. He just put his hands on my chest and pushed me as hard as he could, knocked me flat on my ass. I just lay there on the sidewalk screaming and crying at the top of my lungs, while people, lots of people just walked past me, like I wasn't even there. After awhile, I began to even think that maybe, I wasn't even there. I think I lay there for a few minutes, but at the time it seemed like a few hours, then I remember hearing sirens and seeing a large policeman standing over me. For a second, I thought maybe I should just get up and start running before he maybe, you know, starts beating me up or something, or finds out who I am, and throws me in the Youth Centre. Huh, Oh yeah, I remember now, my friend, his name was, Thomas.

SCENE 2—UNDERNEATCH BRIDGE

POLICE MAN

Hey kid, come on let me help you up, are you ok?

Joe

My friend, my friend Thomas, please help him.

POLICE MAN

I'm afraid there's not much I can do about your friend now, it seems he's been hanging there for a couple of hours, the Paramedics tried to give him CPR, but I'm afraid he's really gone.

Joe

Are you sure? Maybe if they try just one more time, he's my only friend, he's all I've got in this world.

POLICE MAN

Sorry son, I know it must be tough on you, but there is nothing we can do, there's nothing anybody can do for your friend now.

Joe

He tried to tell me last night, but I just wouldn't listen. I told him to stop talking about it. Oh my God, it's all my fault.

POLICE MAN

Come on, let me help you off the ground, you can't lay here all day, come; we'll go sit on that bench over there. We can talk there.

He helped me up and we walked to a park bench nearby. We both sat down and he started talking to me again. I noticed he was carrying a cup of coffee in one of his hand

POLICE MAN

Would you like some coffee, I was just grabbing a cup, when I got this call, it's still warm, I never touched a drop, It might help calm you down.

Joe

For free, I got no money.

POLICE MAN

Yeah, for free, won't cost you anything, here take it.

Joe

I took his coffee and started to drink it down.

POLICE MAN

Listen son, I know it's tough, but you have to know, it's not your fault. I had a friend once who shot himself after his wife left him. I spent a lot of years blaming myself, but the truth is, there was nothing I could do about it, shit like that happens sometimes.

Joe

But he was my friend, the only friend I got. Now what am I gonna do? Why does stuff like this always happen to me?

POLICE MAN

Afraid I can't answer that one, I see a lot of bad things happen, almost every day, because of the job that I have. It's a cruel world sometimes. I know this may be tough for you now, but I need to ask you some questions. I thought I heard you say his name was Thomas, what's his last name.

Joe

I don't know, I never bothered to ask him, I guess I didn't think it was important at the time.

POLICE MAN

Do you know how old he was? When was his birthday?

Joe

I think he was twenty years old, He never talked much about his birthday, he said, as far as he was concerned, he should have never been born, nobody ever celebrated his birthday, so why should he care, never had a birthday cake in his life.

POLICE MAN

Wow, that's pretty sad, how long have you known him?

Joe

Just for a couple of months. I just moved into the area, you know, from up north.

POLICE MAN

Where did he live? What was his address?

Joe

We lived, I mean, he lived, right here, underneath this bridge, he had no address.

POLICE MAN

Do you know where he was from? Where his family was from?

Joe

He said he didn't have any family; he was a foster kid, moved from one foster home to another. He said he was nobodies' child. Never knew what having a real mom and dad was like.

POLICE MAN

That's really sad; I can't imagine not having any family. What's your name?

Joe

Why, are you a cop or something?

POLICE MAN

(Chuckling to himself)
Yeah, I think so; at least I was the last time I checked.

I gave him a fake name.

Joe

Oh yea, I forgot, my name is Lance, Lance Smith.

POLICE MAN

And where do you live Lance Smith?

Joe

I live on Furby Street, 485 Furby, with my mom, my dad died a couple of years ago, suite number 004.

POLICE MAN

I'm sorry to hear that. How long have you and your mom been living there?

Joe

We moved there a couple of months ago.

POLICE MAN

What's your phone number? In case, I need to get a hold of you.

Joe

Don't got a phone, can't afford one.

POLICE MAN

Oh, I see, well, that's about everything I need from you right now, if I have any more questions, I guess I'll have to come to your place.

Joe

No, don't, my mom don't want any cops coming around, she'll yell at me.

POLICE MAN

Sorry, but I may need to ask you more questions, if I do, I'll have to go to your place. Do you need a ride home? I can give you a ride home if you want.

Joe

No thanks, like I said; my mom's don't like cops coming around.

POLICE MAN

Well, here's my card, you can call me anytime, if you think of anything else you could tell us, you know, about you friend Thomas, or, even if you just need to just talk, you know, about him dying, I could find someone you could talk to, there's people out there who do care, believe it or not.

Joe

Thanks, but no thanks, I'll be ok.

POLICE MAN

If you say so, but here, take my card anyway, you know, in case you change your mind

Joe(Facing his body)

I took his card and started to slowly walk away, I was afraid he would ask more questions and maybe find out the truth about me. You know, before that day, I had a low opinion of Cops, but this guy was real nice to me, made me feel a little better, he seemed very kind and caring, I guess not all cops are bad, at least not this one. Hey, why don't you say something? Do I have to do all the talking?

JOE again tries to touch his body.

Joe

You know what; I once had a pair of shoes like that, hey I even had a pair of pants, just like the pair you're wearing, and that shirt, and you know what else, you look just like me, oh my God, you are me. Holy shit, what have I done to myself? What the hell was I thinking? Someone please help me. I've changed my mind, wait, wait, I'll find something to cut me down with, gotta find something, shit, damn, can't find nothing. Gotta get someone to help me. I want to live, I don't want to die.

Joe turns and looks towards the audience, he starts pointing to people and yelling at them.

Joe

Hey you over there, don't just sit there, get the hell up of your effin chair and come and help me. Can't you see I'm dying? What the hell is wrong with you people anyway? Are you just gonna sit there and watch me die? Does anyone of you have a knife or something, to cut me down with? Does anyone out there know how to do CPR? Come on, I'm running out of time, hurry up, before it's too late. Well screw you all then. Aah, never mind, it's too late now, you waited too long. Yeah, that's the way it's always been for me, people only want to help when it's too late. That's the story of my life; you all wait, and talk about it later. Talk is cheap, always talking about what you could have done, or should have done, what you could have said, or should have said. Always trying to sugar coat the issue, well you know what? This is real, this is as real as it gets. So please, don't give me no line about how bad you feel, it's no good to me now. I really don't know how long I hung there. I just remember the dogs leash tightening around my neck. My head started to feel like a ripe tomato, ready to explode off my shoulders and splatter all over the room. I felt my feet start to tingle and get lighter as I swung back and forth like a pendulum on a grandfather clock. My eyes felt like they were two marbles, ready to pop from their sockets. In a few moments, all my life flashed before me, with all its painful memories. Everything was like a movie in a VCR, as if, someone had pushed the fast forward button. I remember thinking, screw you all, eff the world, eff you all. That's when it happened, my spirit started to lift from my body and move me into a world of darkness. In the distance I saw a blinding, bright shining light. I felt myself being drawn to the light, it was soothing and warm and the only emotions I felt were, peace and love. In the distance I saw my people, my ancestors, my grandmothers and grandfathers calling me to the light. In a flash, I was in a different world, a peaceful and caring world, with no pain, no sadness. I never saw such green grass, such blue sky. I don't know how, but I seemed to know everyone, and everyone knew me. I had no needs, no wants, everywhere I looked, it was calm and serene. I wanted to stay there forever. At that moment, a large bird, a giant golden eagle, swooped down and pierced me on the chest with its talons and carried me away back into the darkness. I remember starting to feel pain again as he carried me to another place. It looked like the dark side of the moon. There he let me go; I slowly drifted down to this place and found myself in front a teaching lodge. There was a fire burning brightly inside and I heard a drum beating and someone chanting beautiful peaceful song. I walked towards the entrance of the teaching lodge and looked inside. I saw a grandmother and a grandfather waving at me, to come inside. A part of me really wanted to join them, but I felt I wasn't worthy enough to go inside.

SCENE 4—TEACHING LODGE

GRANDMOTHER

Come in my grandson, you're in a safe place now, there is nothing to be afraid of. Come sit, come join us.

Joe

I'm ashamed to join you; I feel that I've done a bad thing, I've shamed my people.

GRANDMOTHER

No need to feel shame, we're here to only help you, not judge you.

Joe

I dropped to my knees, crawled into the teaching lodge and took my spot in the circle, then the grandfather started talking to me.

GRANDFATHER

You know, the world you came from used to be a good place; we lived in peace and harmony with all living things and were once, a happy people. We were strong, with a spirit that ran proud, like the mighty buffalo that roamed the prairie by the thousands.

Joe

What happened, what changed all that?

GRANDFATHER

Another kind of people came across from the ocean and changed everything. We couldn't figure them out, didn't understand their ways. We did our best to accommodate them, we taught them how to survive, but they seem to have a greedy nature, the more we gave, the more they wanted, the more they took.

Joe

Why did you even bother to help them? Why didn't you chase them away? Just let them die.

GRANDFATHER

That wasn't our nature, not our way. We were taught to share what we had, share Mother Earth. We knew, the world we were living in, was not ours to keep, but a place to find ones true self. We had a job to do, to care for mother earth and everything in it, including those who seem a little backward.

Joe

Huhh, that's putting it mildly.

GRANDMOTHER

Yes, they were strange creatures alright, for some reason, they had the belief that their way was the only way, that they somehow owned mother earth, imagine that, human beings thinking mother earth belonged to them. They even tried to take us captive and make us slaves in their world.

They took us over the ocean and tried to sell us, as they do too many of the animals they've domesticated. They put guns to our heads and told us, if we didn't become slaves, they would kill us.

Joe

What did our people do?

GRANDMOTHER

Our people were very spiritual, we never feared death. We knew, in death we would go to a better place. Our people stood proud and told them, it was a good day to die.

Joe

Then what happened?

GRANDMOTHER

Well you see my grandson, the slave drivers ended up killing them all, you know, we never did make very good slaves.

Joe

I still don't understand, why would our people chose death over life?

GRANDFATHER

Because we believed that if we became slaves, our spirits would die and we would become weak. We knew it was better to die, than to become a slave to anyone. The slave drivers gave up; there was no profit in it for them, because they ended up killing all their cargo.

Joe

Are you telling me that killing yourself is ok?

GRANDFATHER

No, that's not what we are trying to say, we should all strive to live a good life, but only if that life allows you the freedom to become who we are, that way, you stay strong in body, mind and spirit. We could not care for Mother Earth, if we couldn't even care for ourselves. Being a slave is no life at all.

Joe

But what happened then? It seems our people died for nothing, they walk on Mother Earth in shame and without any spirit. You said they would be strong, if they didn't become slaves, I'm confused.

GRANDMOTHER

Because today, we've become a different kind of slave. We've been taught to be a people of greed, we've become like them. We value material gain more than we value ourselves, and if you don't have these things, we begin to believe we are not equal, we walk in shame, we even kill each other in order to gain a sense of having more.

Joe

I thought those kinds of stuff would make us better people.

GRANDMOTHER

It may seem that way, but it made us lose our focus, the center of our being. We became a nation of want, only thinking of ourselves, always wanting more, no matter how much we get, it never seems enough. We no longer live in harmony with nature, or each other.

GRANDFATHER

When you lose your focus, you lose your purpose in life and your spirit dies. You become empty and try to fill the void with addictions, alcohol, drugs, solvents, gambling, sex and religion. We get drunk on God; we become a new kind of slave.

GRANDFATHER

Our people now do very strange things to each other. They have become disconnected; our children have been left to fend for themselves and are in constant search for a home, a family. They judge each other harshly and without mercy, using a religion that's not even theirs. They point fingers and pretend they are holy, claiming their brothers and sisters are nothing but a bunch of hell bound sinners, telling them to sell their possessions, to purchase God's favor.

GRANDMOTHER

But what's even worse, some have been getting our youth hooked on powerful drugs, often forcing them into prostitution on street corners; or order to make a profit. They don't see them as human beings; only as objects to be bought and sold.

Joe

Well, why don't you do something about it? Why do you all continue to ignore the problem?

GRANDFATHER

It's not for us to interfere; all people have the freedom of choice. You take away that freedom, all people will just become like machines or robots. We can only give them choices; they must each choose which path they want to walk on. Many have left the red road.

GRANDMOTHER

We have tried to communicate with them through their dreams, but many of our people have either forgotten how to dream or just choose to ignore them.

Joe

Well, I think that's all a bunch of crap. You have the power to intervene, and you choose to sit back and do nothing. Where were you, when I needed you the most? When I was being beaten and abused. I yelled out, Grandfathers! Grandmothers! Help me! You weren't there, nobody was there.

GRANDMOTHER

Things are not always as they seem. We heard you, we came into your dreams, but you shut us out, like you shut everything and everyone else out, numbed your emotions then tried to get rid of them with drugs and alcohol.

Joe

Well, what else was I suppose to do? My world was all messed up. I had no parents, no family, and no one to turn to.

GRANDFATHER

We understand your anger, we acknowledge your pain, but we tried to show you that there was another way. We put elders in your life, to help you follow the red road, but you refused to listen, you just shut them out and tried to do things your own way.

Joe

Well it's kinda too late now, now what am I suppose to do?

GRANDMOTHER

It's never too late, it only seems that way.

At that moment everything went black again. I was once being lifted and moved to another place. In an instant I was returned to my old apartment, the one I once lived in on Burrows Ave. This time though, it was very different. All the walls seemed dark and gloomy, as if all the paint had somehow been scraped off and everything was covered in a musty grey dust. The windows were so dirty, no light would shine through. There were mice running all over the place. Although, I hated being there, I didn't want to leave, because, somehow, I felt safe there. I was well hidden and protected from the cruel world outside. I was in total darkness, except for small bit of light that shone through a small crack at the bottom of my front door. I somehow knew it was a very beautiful day, but I didn't want to go outside. I wanted to stay in my darkened world forever. All of a sudden my door swung open and a very bright and blinding light came into the room. I saw a man standing in the doorway and beams of very bright light surrounded his entire form. At first, I couldn't see who this person was, for a moment, I thought I had somehow seen Jesus himself. I rubbed my eyes and looked again, this time; I saw who it really was. It was my friend Thomas. Thomas started waving his hands as if he wanted me to follow him into the light.

SCENE 5—APARTMENT DOORWAY

Joe

Thomas is that really you? How did you get here?

Thomas

Never mind that man, please listen to me.

Joe

What do you want from me? Why are you here?

Thomas

Come on man, you can't stay here in this darkness, you need to come into the light.

Joe

But I don't want to come into the light; I don't ever want to see the outside world again.

Thomas

But you have to; this is no way to live your life, is no life.

Joe

You should talk, coming from some who bailed out on me when the going got too rough, why did you do that to me? Why did you become like everyone else in my life, I loved, abandoning me, never sticking around, not there when I needed you most?

Thomas

Listen, I know, what I did was not right, at the time I really didn't think I had any other choice, but I never meant to hurt you, I was just, in so much pain, so much was wrong in my life and I didn't know how to fix it. I guess, I took, what I thought at the time, was the only way out.

Joe

You know, I spent years missing you, I would often walk to that bridge hoping that by some strange miracle, I would see you again, but that never happened. How could you? And now you're here, trying to give me advice.

Thomas

You have the right to be angry with me, you even have a right to hate me, and I'm sorry, but I can't change the past, can't undo what I did to myself, but I'm here now, I want to help you.

Joe

How can you help me? Your dead, what can a dead person do for me?

Thomas

Come on man, you gotta face it.

Joe

Face what? What you talking about?

Thomas

You know what I'm talking about, all that stuff you been running all your life from, all that stuff that has stopped you from living, kept you in a world of darkness.

Joe

I still don't know what you're talking about.

Thomas

You know, the people in your life who hurt you, all that sexual abuse.

Joe

How do you know about that? I never said nothing to you about that.

Thomas

You know, in this world you can't hide nothing, on earth you waste a lot of energy hiding from the truth, here, there is only the truth, everything becomes revealed, you have to face it, you got no choice, if you want to find your center, you know, become whole again.

Joe

I really don't know if I can, there's so much to deal with, way too much pain.

Thomas

Sure you can, you're really a strong person, you see things that must people wouldn't even comprehend, you have a strong will.

Joe

Thomas, will you be there, you know, to help me through it, I need you to help me.

Thomas

I'll be there but only in spirit, well I gotta go now.

Joe

Is this another one of your painful goodbyes?

Thomas

You know, there's no such thing as goodbye, even in death, we meet again in the afterlife. That's why, in the Ojibway language, there's no word for goodbye, our people always said, igawabamin Apii, which means, I'll see you later.

Joe

No, please, Thomas don't leave me, I don't want you to leave me; ever again.

Thomas

But I have to leave, go back to where I came from, see ya.

Chris Beach

Joe

No Thomas, come back, no, please come back, no,
Thomas, I love you.

*As Thomas turned around and started to leave, I
noticed a bright, blinding light in the distance.
At first I thought it might be the sun in the
horizon, but this light was a lot brighter than
the sun. Thomas started to run towards the light
and I ran after him begging him to come back,
but he never did turn around and stop. Like a
flash, he faded into the light until he became
one with the light. You know, since the day,
Thomas hung himself underneath that bridge, I
always wondered if he ended up in a bad place,
but after I saw him run into that light; I
somehow knew that he was in a very good place
and that someday I would see him again. I tried
my best to also run to the light, but it seemed
a long way off in the distance. For some reason,
I believed I must always try to move closer to
this light, that I may never get there, but every
day, I will be a little bit closer to it. I'm not
sure how long I followed the light, sometimes
I ran and sometimes I walked. It was the most
beautiful day I had ever seen. Everything was so
peaceful, everything so bright and colourful.
I came upon a meadow with a babbling brook, I
decided to sit and rest for a while, before I
continued my journey to the light. I knelt down
to look into the water and cupped my hands to
get a drink. In the reflection I saw myself and
then two other people standing above me, a young
man and a young woman. I jumped up and turned
around to see who they were. It was Susan and
Joseph; my mother and father. Although I don't*

remember seeing my mother before, I knew it was her.

SCENE 6—MEADOW NEAR A BROOK

Joe

Mother, Father, is that really you?

Susan

Yes my son, it is us, we've come to see you.

Joe

Oh my God, all my life I've always wanted to meet you, see what you looked like, and now here you are. You're so beautiful, so lovely. And you my father, you look so different, so much younger, so healthy.

Joseph

Yes my son, we're in a different place now, a whole new world, we're in a good place, a place of never ending peace and love.

Joe

Father, the last time I so you, you look so beaten, so roughed up. I was so ashamed of you,

I didn't want to know you, I didn't want to be your son.

Joseph

Well, I don't blame you; it must have been very hard on you seeing me the way I was. I guess I wasn't much of a father to you, not much of anything, I had no spirit, no will to live. I felt I had nothing to live for.

Joe

What about me? Was I nothing to you too?

Joseph

You know, when you let the pain consume you, that's all you feel, it's not that I didn't love you, it's, I just couldn't feel anything else, I couldn't feel those good feelings, like happiness and love.

Susan

We're very sorry Joe, for not being there for you, when you really needed us. I thought having you would bring me and your father closer together, I wanted so much for my life to be, I don't know, at least maybe better than watching my dad beating up on my mom. I felt, I the compelling need to somehow get out, and I thought your father would be my ticket. I never meant to hurt you.

Joe

Didn't you even love me, at least enough to stop what you were doing, to try and make a better life for me. Why did you abandon me?

Susan

Honest Joe, I really tried, I thought about you every day, I just didn't have anyone to help me, anyone to turn too. You know, evils spirits live in alcohol, when you take it into your body, the spirits take over your mind and soul, they make you do things, you wouldn't otherwise do.

Joe

So you just gave up on me, gave up on yourself, that's a bunch of bull, you know how long, I longed for you to come and get me, everyday looking out my window, wishing you would come and take me away, take me home. All I ever wanted was, to go home.

Susan

I tried to get you back, even went into some treatment centers, but my social worker kept telling me, I would never see you again. I guess, I just gave up trying.

Joe

Oh, cry me a river. Is that the best you can say?

Susan

Powerful demons live in the drugs I started taking. At first, they made me feel better, helped me cope with everything, then they starting to suck every bit of self worth I had. When I tried to stop taking them, those demons would constantly haunt every inch of my being. I wasn't strong enough to fight them.

Joe

And what about you; my great and wonderful father, did you give up on me too? Was I not worth the time of day; not worth fighting for?

Joseph

I went to see your social worker, to ask about you, she just laughed at me, told me to leave or she would have me arrested. I made some bad choices, made some mistakes, I just didn't know what else, I could do.

Joe

So, I was just another one of your bad choices; another one of your so called mistakes.

Joseph

It wasn't like that, I never saw you as a mistake,
I was the one who screwed it all up. If I could
take it all back, I would, start all over again,
I might have at least, made things better for
you, and your mom.

Susan

Listen Joe, you've got to at least try and forgive
us, we messed up big time with you, and we are
really sorry, but, we can't undo the past, you
have to let it go.

Joe

Forgive you; forgive him, after all you've done to
me, you were suppose to take care of me, everything
I've been through, never, I won't forgive you;
you two don't deserve my forgiveness.

Susan

You know Joe; resentment is like a bad form
of cancer, a sickness that invades every inch
of your being, strips you of all your energy,
blackens your spirit, eats away at you until
there's nothing left. That's what happened to
me and your father, resentment stopped us from
living, that's why we became alcoholics and drug
addicts, to try and control the rage living
inside us. Yes, you have every right to be angry
at your father and me, even to the point of
hating us, but you are the one, who will lose

in the end. Don't let it destroy you, like it destroyed us. Let it go, please, I'm begging you. Forgiveness is something you must do, not for the sake of your father and me, but for the sake of yourself. It's the only way out, Maano.

Joe

I began screaming and crying at them, yelling my lungs out. I turned away from my mother and father for only a moment, put my arm in front of my face to cover my eyes, I was so angry with them, I didn't want to see them no more, and when I took my arm away and turned around again, they were gone. Always doing that to me, leaving without a word of goodbye. I screamed for them to come back, I felt their abandonment all over again, I was crying and pleading, begging them to show themselves, but they were gone, like they were never even there. Then, I started pondering over the last word my mother said to me, maano. Maano, what the hell is that? What did she mean maano? Then, I remembered a time when I was in that youth institution for about three years. An elderly woman was invited in to talk to us, give us that teaching. She sat us in a circle and made us smudge with sweetgrass. All the while I kept thinking, this is stupid, there's no God, what a bunch of crap.

SCENE 7—CIRCLE WITH A GROUP OF YOUNG BOYS AND AN ELDERLY WOMAN

ELDERLY WOMAN

Booshoo, My name is Blue Thunderbird Woman. I'm honoured to be here today, and sit with you. In my hand, I am holding a braid of one of our four sacred medicines, its called sweetgrass. I am lighting the sweetgrass, and I am going to smudge with it. When I am done, I will pass it, and you will all, in turn, smudge yourselves. First, you smudge your hands to cleanse them, then you smudge your minds to have good thoughts, then you smudge your ears to hear good things, then you smudge your eyes to see good things, then you smudge your mouth, in order to say good things, then you smudge your heart so that your hearts will become pure, then you smudge your body, to cleanse your spirit, your whole being. Now it's your turn, when you are done; pass it on to the next person.

Joe

The sweetgrass was passed around to everyone, and when it came to me, I quickly smudged myself just to get it over with.

Blue Thunderbird Woman

In my hand, I am now holding an eagle feather. In this circle, two things need to happen, they are caring and sharing. The person holding the eagle feather, is the one who does the sharing, during this time, your job is to listen with a caring ear. If you choose not to listen, the message you give the person, who is holding the feather is, that you don't care what they have to say. You demonstrate caring, by listening. In some of our homes and families, we often were not listened too, we were given the message, that what we have to say, was not important, and then we began to feel, we ourselves, were not important. I don't want any one of you, leaving this circle today, feeling you are not important, so everyone please listen. When the eagle feather comes to you, sound your name to let everyone know that you are here, you are a part of God's creation and you exist. Speak your mind, say meegwetch, which means thank you, and pass it on.

Joe

After she spoke, she then sent the eagle feather around and everyone got a turn to say something, some were even stupid enough, to tell everyone, about what was bothering them. The sickest part was, when some of them even started crying. Me, I never said nothing, just my name and I passed it on. Don't need any of this devil stuff.

Blue Thunderbird Woman

Now I'm going to tell you a story about my grandmother. She was born in the Cote Indian Reservation, in the year 1886. This reservation was in the province of Saskatchewan. When she was a little girl, her father died and her mother, my great-grandmother remarried and moved to Manitoba. When she was about 16 years of age, she married my grandfather. Life was hard for her; the man she married was an alcoholic, he would often get drunk and beat her. She had a total of

10 children. 5 of them died from TB. As a little girl, what I remember most about my grandmother was her smiling face. She always seemed so full of life. I often wondered how and where, she got her strength from. So, one day I asked her. Of all the hard times that you've been through, how come you're not angry and bitter? My grandmother told me, you know, the world can be a very cold and uncaring place. There are many people who seem to take pleasure, seeing you fall. You can't let things like that get the best of you. You just have to smile, and say to yourself, maano. Maano is an Ojibway word meaning, "Let it go or, let it be". Forgive people who have hurt you and you will free yourself to live a good life. Because of my grandmother, every time I struggle with things in life, I have little or no control over, I always think of her teachings, and say to myself maano. You know, it's carried me through many hard times in life, so now, I'm passing my grandmothers teaching on to you, in hopes, that someday, it will help you, the way it has helped me. My grandmother entered the spirit world in 1989, she was 103 years old. I believed she lived such a long life, because she truly lived by the word, maano.

Joe

I kept thinking to myself, what a bunch of bull crap, forgive, that's easy for her to say, she doesn't know what I've been through, she doesn't know what was done to me, she can shove her maano up her bum. In my mind, I kept saying, kigeet, kigeet, your big fat bum, I don't need this crap, I don't need anyone.

I turned and started walking again, not really knowing where I was going, all the while I was wishing my mother and father would come to me again. Maybe I shouldn't have said all those things to them. Maybe I should have just been happy they were with me. Then, sometimes I would remember stuff, and become angry with them again. It's all their fault, just two effin losers; I hope they choke on each other's tears. But, the truth was, I really longed to be with them, find them again, they were my parents, my family, no matter what they may have done in the past. Then, I began seeing that bright blinding light again in the distance. Then, what I thought was a man, came from that direction. It wasn't really a man; it was more like a glow of energy that came gently close to me. I felt as if, I was a part of that energy.

SCENE 8—PATH

Joe

Who are you? What are you?

ENERGY

I've been called many things, been given many names, I am what I am.

Joe

What do you want from me?

ENERGY

It's not, what I want from you, but, what you want of me.

Joe

What do you mean? Now I'm really confused.

ENERGY

Many times, I've heard you cry out to me in anger, when things didn't seem to go the way, you wanted them to.

Joe

You mean you're, you know, the Big Guy. The one and only, worshipped by many people, all over the world.

ENERGY

Like I said, I've been called many things, been given many names, but I never intended for people to worship me. When I walked on Mother Earth, and showed myself, I asked the people to follow my example, to love one another. I didn't come to be worshipped; but to be followed, to be a helper

Joe

Well, I never felt love from any of them, all they seem to wanted to do was, condemn me, tell me how bad I was, and money, they were forever asking for money, they never helped me.

ENERGY

Yes, there are many blind people out there, who see only what they want to see, don't want to hear the truth. You know, before I walked the earth, they were even stoning pregnant woman, killing them, and their unborn children, and yet, they had a commandment, not to kill. Today, they use a different kind of stone, to hurt each other; they stone them with their tongues. They judge without mercy, and then ask mercy from me. They pray to me, but refuse to hear me, only want answers to suit themselves.

Joe

What about me? Why haven't you ever answered me? Why didn't you ever come, when I called?

ENERGY

Of course I was there, I've always listened to you, I bled for you, and suffered with you. I've even died for you, it's you, who won't put your faith in me, you lack faith.

Joe

I tried to have faith, wanted so much to believe, but you've never done nothing for me, never helped me.

ENERGY

It only seems that way, but, I've done great things for you.

Joe

Like what? You gave me a rotten life, you gave me, alcoholic drug addicted Indians for parents. Why didn't you give me, white sober parents, with lots of money? Parents, I could be proud of, so I could have a good life, so I wouldn't have to walk in shame.

ENERGY

You know, many people have a great deal of money, but only pretend to be happy. Some even sit on millions of dollars, while their own people die of starvation. They think, they're fooling me, but they're only fooling themselves. Rich parents are no guarantee, you will live a good life. The parents you were blessed with were chosen by you, long before you were born. It was not I.

Joe

What are you talking about? Why would I choose such awful parents? You're a liar. My mother was a drunk, and my father was a butt picking bum. Anybody would have to be insane, to want to have parents like that.

ENERGY

Your mother and father loved you, no matter what they were, and they still do.

Joe

(Dropping to his knees crying)

No, no, they never loved me, never took care of me. The only thing they loved was drugs and alcohol. I just wanted them to, take care of me, to love me, they couldn't even do that. I hate them for the stinking life I had. They could have made things different, better. But no, they just wanted to party and have a good time. I hate them. How could you even think they loved me? Nobody loved me.

ENERGY

Who you are, stems from your experiences. Life is full of experiences, good and bad. You can learn from them, or you can let them destroy you, it's all up to you. You wanted to be taken through an experience; you wanted to know what, that kind of life would be like.

Joe

You mean, what do you mean?

ENERGY

How can you appreciate the good in life, if you've never experienced the bad? You were sent to the earth with nothing and you leave with nothing, even your own body is left behind. Only the things you learn, will live forever, make you the person that you become.

Joe

Seems to me, there is a lot of bad things and no good things. Why don't you do something about it?

ENERGY

I did, I made you. Oh, there are plenty of good on Mother Earth; you just have to look for it. Have you ever stopped to listen to the birds sing, the Wind blow? Saw and felt the power of the Thunder and Lightning, when the Thunderbirds clap their wings. There are many good, truly kind people in the world. You wasted your life trying to please people who never cared about you; tried so hard to get them to like you. And, you ignored the ones who really did care about you.

                          Joe

Like who, who you talking about?

                        ENERGY

Like that policeman underneath that bridge, he
really wanted to help.

                          Joe

Well excuse me, is that suppose to make me feel
better?

                        ENERGY

I have given you everything you need.

                          Joe

Like what, Indians have nothing, no pride, no
money, and no self-worth.

                        ENERGY

Your people have plenty, their medicines, their
elders, sweat lodges, Sundance's, and their
bundles, everything they need.

Joe

But, I've always thought those things were not right, that they were somehow, evil.

ENERGY

Evil, is only what lives in the hearts and minds of the ignorant. I have given all people gifts, it's up to you, if want to use them, or not, pick up your bundles, in them, lives your pride.

Joe

But, it's too late for me; I've done something terrible to myself.

ENERGY

It's never too late; you must go back and return to your people. Teach them how to become human beings again, teach them to take back their pride, help free them from their addictions.

Joe

No, never. I never want to go back to that place. I want to stay here; you can't make me go back, not ever.

ENERGY

But you must go back, take back Mother Earth.

Joe

We can't take back Mother Earth; it's too late, someone else owns Mother Earth.

ENERGY

Nobody can own Mother Earth.

Joe

Anyway, what will we do with all the other races? You know, the whites, the blacks, and the people from Asia, they will never agree to leave.

ENERGY

When I say, take back Mother Earth, I don't mean to get rid of everyone else. For a long time your people have been made to feel, that they have no right to live on Mother Earth, that they are somehow aliens in their own land. They must take back the right to breathe the same air as everyone else, the right to live a good life, to be happy and proud of who they are, have the belief; they have every right to be there. When they do this, Mother Earth will truly belong to them again.

Joe

But I don't want to go back, why I can't stay here with you?

ENERGY

Because, you must go back, you still have things on Mother Earth you need to do.

Joe

Will I be able to communicate with you, you know, when things get too much for me to handle.

ENERGY

I was always there, in many different forms. Just look for me and you will find me in every living thing, every rock, and every blade of grass. You will be given many gifts, use them wisely. Offer your tobacco every day, talk to your elders, and pray, you talk, I'll listen.

SCENE 9—STAGE

Joe (Addressing the audience)

You know, to this day, I'm still not sure how long I hung there, was it a few days, a few hours, a few minutes or, a few seconds? I do remember looking away from the energy and seeing myself hanging in that basement. Then I saw three little people come towards my lifeless body. Two of them grabbed my feet and began lifting me up. The third one, looked like he was carrying a knife. He climbed up to my shoulders and started cutting the dog's leash. The leash let go and I fell to the basement floor. My spirit, returned to my body and I could feel myself breath as my heart started beating again. I came to for a few seconds and managed to pull myself up to the top of the stairs. I remember pushing the door open and collapsing on the kitchen floor. I was told that someone called an ambulance and I was rushed to the nearest hospital. They say I lay in a coma for the next three days. The next thing I remember, I came too and a nurse was standing over me adjusting my intervenes. I could feel myself breathe; I could hear my heart beating. I kept thinking to myself, oh my God; I've been given second chance.

A black faceless figure comes from the background where he has been standing the whole time. He takes the shape of a man starts moving around Joe like a snake.

Energy

You know, suicide is a spirit who will come and whisper in your ear, usually, when you are at your lowest point in life. Some people think he's an evil spirit; some even go as far as calling him, the devil himself. Like this guy dancing around Joe, trying desperately to convince him to do himself in. He's the one everyone is afraid of, the one nobody wants to talk about, the one everyone tries to ignore. All I can tell you is, he definitely is a spirit, because I've heard him many a times in my own life. He will often speak to you in a low sadistic voice, trying to convince you that killing yourself is better than trying to live. He will tell you such things as, nobody loves you, and nobody cares about you, over and over again until you begin to believe it.

(Joe sits in chair writhing as black figure whispers in the shadows behind him)

He tells you all your worries and pains will all go away, that the people who have hurt you in life will suffer, after you are gone. Kill yourself; it's the only way out.

(Joe sits in chair writhing, screaming "No")
But, you know what he doesn't tell you, that if you kill yourself, there is no coming back. You can't later say, I've changed my mind, I want to live. Once you're dead, you're dead, and the people you will hurt the most, are the people who really do love you, your Grandmothers and Grandfathers, your moms and dads, your brothers and sisters, your nieces and nephews, and your close friends, your spouse and, your children. They will spend the rest of their lives wondering about, why you did it. Some may never get over it, and some, my even do it themselves. The children you could have had will never exist. Suicide is really saying to you, I have no right to be here, breathe the same air as everyone else, my existence doesn't matter. So, if the spirit of suicide every tries to whisper in your ear, and tries to get you to kill yourself, tell him, kigeet, your butt. Tell him to get lost. And, if he still doesn't leave, tell him to eff off. Tell him, I'm here; I have a right to be here, and I'm gonna stay here.

(Joe stands up defiant, proud.. and black figure recedes back into background)

Joe

If you are confused and in a lot of pain, go find someone to talk to, someone who will listen, and not try and tell you to not talk Like that. Suicide lives in silence, and the more you talk about it, the better you will start to feel, and the stronger you will get. It will lessen the chance of you actually doing it. Suicide will loosen its grip on you. You've got to stop blaming everyone for the way your life has turned out, for the way you are feeling. When you blame, you give up your power to change. There are good people in the world who will listen; you just have to find them. You can even look in the phone book. Nothing will change in your life, unless you take the time to find people, who will help. You're not alone you know, most people have thought about suicide, at least once in their lifetime, but not everyone does it. When you start talking, you will find out there are many people just like you. Nothing is as bad as you may think it is. For Joe, He got lucky; he was given a second chance. Most people who try to commit suicide succeed. They don't get a second chance. Don't give the spirit of suicide any power, fight to live, learn to be strong, and do your best to live a good life. Be proud of who you are, and if anyone tries to take that from you, remember what you say to them, kigeet.

Indian Joe Blow—Part 3

"Black Eagle Thunderbird Man"

Cast of characters

1. Joe
2. Elder
3. Frank
4. Old Man
5. Native Foster Mom
6. Foster Sister
7. Lodge Conductor
8. Scar face
9. Second Youth
10. Daniel
11. Younger Man
12. John
13. Dog Owner
14. Little People (no lines, not seen)
15. Three silent youth, (no lines)

SCENE 1—Pipestone Quarry

Joe is inside a pipe stone quarry in Pipestone Minnesota. It's a very hot day, and he his sweating and almost passing out from the heat. He is with an older man, an Aboriginal elder, and they are working together trying to break solid rock with chisels and sledge hammers. Joe holds the chisel in one hand and attempts strike it with a smaller sludge hammer. He catches has thumb between the hammer and the chisel. Joe screams.

Joe

Damn man, damn it.

Elder

You know, this is a sacred placed. You really should try not to swear here.

Joe

Well hell, man, I just smashed my effin thumb, it really hurts.

Joe pulls off his glove and throws it on the ground. His thumb is throbbing, bleeding and blood drips on the ground. Joe puts his thumb in his mouth and starts sucking on it. Once in a while he pulls it out and looks at it, to see if it's still bleeding. The elder looks at the blood on the ground and pulls out his hanky and wipes the blood up and turns to Joe showing Joe the blood on the hanky.

Elder

You know the old ones say that the pipe stone we are looking for was mad from the blood of our ancestors. Many years ago, many of our people we slaughtered here and their blood flowed like a mighty river.

Sediments settled on top of their blood and formed these mighty rocks were and trying to remove. The weight of these rocks compressed our people's blood and they too turned to stone. That's what the pipe stone is red, from the blood of our people.

Joe

Yeah, well it all looks the same to me.

Elder

No, this rock is different from the rest of the rock, pipestone is a softer rock. It's a rock that can be shaped and formed with small sharp tools. For many years now, we've been using it to form the bowls of our sacred pipes. The bowl is what we call the female. The stem is what we call the male. We carve the stem of the pipe from a certain type of tree; I prefer to use wood from the ash tree. It has a soft center, can easily be cleaned out using a heated wire. When we put the female and male part together they create a balance in the universe. Helps us communicate with our maker, the creator of all things, God.

Joe

If you say so old man.

Elder

It's true, that's why the world is so messed up, and we don't have balance in our lives. Our men an woman have forgotten or how to get along with Each other, why so many of our children are in Foster care, it's the children that suffer when there is no balance.

Joe

Well, that's nice old man. Now my blood is all over the place too. Where do you come up with these stupid stories anyway?

Elder

They're not just stupid stories, these stories have been passed on down for many generations, to help our young people through life. The trouble is our young people don't listen to our elders no more. They don't value our old ones.

Joe

Well what the heck do you expect, have you seen some of our elders lately? You should come back with me to Winnipeg, to Main Street, up north, on the reserves. You'll change your mind about listening to the elders in a hurry.

Elder

You know, I used to be one of those people on Main Street. Drinking anything I could get my hands on. I know all about them, I was one of them.

Joe

Wow, I never would have guessed.

Elder

Yeah, I was very lost alright, didn't know who I was, what my purpose was. I guess I must have been pretty pitiful at the time.

Joe

So how did you end up here, in this place?

Elder

Same as you I guess, trying to find myself, trying to find some meaning from it all.

Joe

Well, I think this really sucks shit. We've be here for seven fricken days now, and all we've managed to do is remove a few small chunks of this shit, It's going to take us a couple of months at lease to get to the bottom.

Elder

Well, things could be worse, our people used to mine these quarries with homemade tools and rocks, they didn't have any fancy chisels or store bought 16 pound sledge hammers. I tell you, they must have been some tough people.

Joe

When I was told to come here and get my pipe, I thought one would be waiting for me. All I had to do was come and pick one up. Man what the hell are we doing here? I should be at home sipping back on some nice ice cold beer, not dying here in this heat, drinking piss warm stinking water.

Elder

Sure it's tough here, but from what I've learned in life, nothing good in life comes easy. You gotta work at it a little at a time.

Joe

Yeah I was told, listen to your dreams, you will be given many gifts. This is no fricken gift to me. Something you have to work your fricken ass off for. You know what a real gift is; that welfare check that that government gives me at the end of the month. Two hundred and fourteen dollars don't even have to give them the sweat off my brows. Now that's I gift if I ever seen one.

Elder

That's no gift, that's just a dumb hand out. You know, our people were never welfare people, we never took unless we gave something first. Even when we went hunting, we would offer up our tobacco and speak to the spirit of that animal. Apologize for taking its life, and thanking it for giving up its life so that we may live. We would return to our camp and the woman would work to prepare the hunt for the day. And for those who may have not done well on the hunt, they were told to come and help themselves.

Joe

Sounds like welfare to me, dependency in its purest form. I guess that's where our people learned it from.

Elder

No, it's not like that. Not like the teachings of the Medicine Wheel.

Joe

Now what the heck is a Medicine Wheel? Oh, never mind, forget I asked.

Elder

It's what our people used to live by, before our way of life got interrupted. It is the four quadrants of the circle of life.

Joe

I told you forget about it old man, you're just going to end up giving me a bigger headache than I already have.

Elder

You know, the Medicine Wheel teaches us that there is really only one time in life that we are truly dependent on others for survival. Except I guess when you get real old and your mind starts to go, and your bodies plumbing starts to malfunction. You become child like again. That's the first stage, the infant stage. Some people never learn to move beyond that stage, get stuck there somehow, like they never grow up.

Joe

Why you looking at me when you say that, I never had anyone look after me, had to grow up real fast.

Elder

We'll anyway; the second stage is where most of our young people are really stuck in, the co-dependent stage.

Joe

What the heck does that mean, co-dependent stage?

Elder

That's when we believe that we need to have someone in our lives to live or we will die. Like when a person stays in an abusive relationship because they think they can't live without that other person. Many times they even kill themselves when their partner leaves the relationship because they think their life is somehow not worth living anymore. That stage is also called the adolescent stage.

Joe

You mean just like I tried to do?

Elder

The third stage is called the independent stage. It's actually the opposite of co-dependency, when people come to believe that they don't need anybody. Go to the other extreme, usually because they may have been let down too many times by the people closest in their lives.

Joe

And what's wrong with that? I too couldn't depend on anybody. I learned fast not to trust nobody, ef them, for all I cared they could all rot in hell. Yes, I came to the conclusion that I needed no one; Joe Blow was on his own.

Elder

You know, you ever wonder how some people get so lonely, in a world that has six billion people in it.

Joe

I don't know, I guess they can't find anyone.

Elder

No, part of the reason is because they have become so independent, that they close up and shut others out; won't let people in.

Joe

Been hurt too many times, too afraid I guess.

Elder

That's true, but at the same time, nothing is a guarantee in life, if you don't learn how to trust, you will live one sad pathetic life. Sure there is a chance you might get hurt, but you will never know otherwise. You know, at one time, I believed I was so independent that when I did need help, I couldn't bring myself to even ask.

Joe

So what's left then, there is nothing left, black or white, right or wrong, co-dependent or Independent?

Elder

The way our people used to live, you can't see the world as just black or white, right or wrong. There is another way.

Joe

And what is that old man?

Elder

The final stage called inter-dependence. When we come to realize that we do need one another, we do need others in our life, for compionship, help or just for company, to have someone around to talk to every now and then, a friend. This is better known as the Elder stage.

Joe

I tried to have friends; most just took and never gave, like the people in your story that came for the meat the other hunters killed.

Elder

No, in return, they would do the same for others on days when others got nothing. You know many people see Indians as welfare people, who all we do is take, take, and take. If that were true, we would be wealthy. The truth is, the real takers in the world are the very rich who take until there is nothing left, while the rest of the people are forced to do without or starve to death. No, all our people really wanted was to have just enough as to live day to day. We were never people of greed.

Joe

There you go again with another one of your bullshit stories. Man your good; you should become a politician or something, always bullshitting.

Elder

These stories are no bullshit. We were once a free nation lived off the land. Everything was provided for us from the land. Things like our food, our clothing, our tools, and even our medicines.

Joe

So, what happened then, old wise one?

Elder

It was the government who turned us into welfare people. They wanted our land, our resources; they wanted to build a country by forgetting about the people who were already here. They tried building a railroad across our land. Our people saw that and started ripping up the tracks. The government became annoyed and angered.

Joe

Yeah right. Our people never stood for nothing.

Elder

Well, the government knew that they couldn't pay us off with money, and they also knew our main source of food came from the buffalo.

So, they went and killed off nearly all the buffalo, thousands and thousands of them until they almost became extinct.

Joe

So, that still doesn't make us welfare people.

Elder

Without the buffalo, our main food source, many of our people died from starvation. We gave in to signing treaties with the government in exchange for food rations every month. That's how the government turned our people into welfare people, so if we didn't behave and accept their policies, they would take away our food. We became wards of the state. They made us welfare people to have power and control over us.

Joe

Wow, I never thought of it that way.

Joe picks looks at his thumb, bends down and picks up his glove and puts it on, picks up his hammer and chisel and both men continue working. They work for a while until Joes frustration level goes up and he once again begins to talk to the elderly man who is with him.

Joe

You know, we don't have to do this.

Elder

Do what?

Joe

Break up all this stinking rock. We could leave and go back to the trading post store and buy some pipe stone. It's only three dollars a pound. There are lots. Nobody will ever know. I won't say nothing if you won't.

Elder

But you'll know and I'll know. I have a permit to mine here for the rest of this month. I'll make you a deal, if we don't find any pipestone by the time the permit runs out, then I'm sure the grandfathers won't mind if we go buy it. After all, we did put in the work for it.

Joe

I guess, but it would be so much easier if we just stopped right now. I've never worked so hard in all my life, even working for that roofing company in Winnipeg wasn't as hard as what we're doing now.

Elder

I know, but let's, give it a try anyway.

Joe

Man, why do I have to do everything the hard way. You know some people they seem to get stuff by just asking an elder and getting what they want. All they had to do was pass tobacco. Once I wanted to know what Clan I was from, so I went to a sweat lodge in East Selkirk. The woman before me was told right then and there, you know what they said to me?

Elder

What did they say?

Joe

They told me, I had to go out into the bush, put my food and water away for four days, and I would find out what Clan I was from. I was so pissed off. Man as if I had nothing better to do with my life.

The elder smiled at Joe.

Elder

So, what did you do?

Joe

What you smiling about. It's not funny you know.

Elder

Nothing, so did you?

Joe

At first, I wasn't going to do nothing, I thought to myself, who cares what the hell my clan was, don't need it anyway. They can shove it, where the sun doesn't shine. Then for some strange reason, I just had to find out, like I was being haunted by it.

Elder

Tell me about it.

Joe

I went to this house in the north end; I was told a man lived there who specialized in taking people out into the bush. His name was Lightning Strikes Twice. I called him Lighting for short. I passed him my tobacco and told him who I was and what I wanted. He prepared me for what I needed and on the next long weekend, he took me out into the bush. In the bush he made me prepare a makeshift tent and he put to sticks in front. He said he was going to leave me there and come and check on me every day. He told me to cross the two sticks in front of the doorway to let him know when I was done, and then he would come and take me out. He then left me there and went away. The first night was ok; I had a lot of liquids and food before I went into the tent. I went to sleep not long after he left and only woke a few times in the night. You hear strange noises in the night, and they make your mind think strange things. The next day was a little rough. No body to talk too, nobody around to listen to you. Your own thoughts become amplified and you try to convince yourself to quit and go home. I fell asleep in the evening and woke up sometime during the night. I was thirsty and I thought I would die of starvation. I heard strange noises coming from outside as if some was walking around outside.

Scene 2

Inside make shift tent. Joe hears someone walking around outside.

Joe

Who's there? Is that you lightning?

No one answers but the sounds get louder.

Joe

I said who's there? What do you want? Stop kidding around, tell me who you are.

Joe begins to get scared and starts yelling out.

Joe

I've got a gun you know, you don't fricken get away from here. I'll kill you, I mean it, I will kill you.

The footsteps get even louder and louder and they sound like there are now a few people running around the tent. Joe's fear starts to overcome him, he begins crying.

Joe

I'm warning you, go away, please go away, hell man, go away.

Joe picks up a stick up off the ground from inside the tent.

Joe

I've got a weapon in my hands you know. Leave me alone, I'm warning you.

Joe starts hitting the side of the tent with the stick yelling.

Joe

Go away; get the hell out of here.

All of a sudden it gets deadly quiet outside. Joe sits back and breathes a sigh of relief.

Joe

Yeah, just get lost, and don't come back, if you know what's good for you. You bunch of chicken shits.

Just then you hear the sound of what sounds like the sound of someone beating on the outside of the tent with a stick. Joe hits the inside of the tent with his stick.

Joe

I told you to leave me alone, why don't you just go away and leave me alone.

Then it sounds like hundreds of sticks are hitting the outside of his tent. Joe huddles close to the ground in terror. He begins screaming and crying covering his hears with both hands.

Joe

No, no, leave me alone, why are you doing this to me?

Joe retreats into the fetal position crying at the top of his lungs.

Joe

Oh mommy, oh daddy, help me. Mommy, mommy, ahhhh, help me, please help me.

Outside the banging continues, but this time it continues with the laughter if little children, as if they are playing and having fun. Joe just continues screaming and crying on the ground, calling mommy, daddy. Joe falls sleep and doesn't wake until the next morning. He opens the doorway to his tent and looks outside.

Joe

Man what a trip I had last night, your emotions sure know how to mess with your mind. I was really tripping there for a while. I'm so glad its daylight now. One more night, and I could go home. Maybe I should go home know, Oh what I would do for a nice cold glass of water. I'm so hungry I can barely move. It's such a nice day today, the sun is shining, birds are singing. Man what the heck am I doing here? Why do I do this to myself? Make myself suffer, haven't I suffered enough, Man I should just cross the poles and get lightning to get me out of here. Maybe he's gone and will never come back; maybe he's just like everyone else who has abandoned me, Left me here to die. Even if I wanted, I probably wouldn't know how to get back home. What if he doesn't come back? Then what am I going to do? Damn, why did I bother to come here, all hungry and thirsty. I hate this place, I want to go home. Man Lightning, where the hell are you? You're supposed to take care of me? You promised you'd help me. I wonder what time it is. Man time here seems to pass so slow, just like in some of those foster homes I was in, you wait, don't really know what you're waiting for, but you wait anyway. Now here I am playing the waiting game, waiting for something to happen. Probably nothing's going to, nothing at all. Maybe I'm just fooling myself, wanting so bad to believe in something, anything. Is God real? God if you're listening, if you are, send me a big Mac with a large order of fries, and an ice cold cola, super sized. Come on God, they say you can do anything. Or are you going to be just like some of my foster parents, never buying me anything. Yeah they would buy their own kids, but me, I'd get nothing. A big Mac and fries, that's not to much to ask for, is it? Look, I going to close my eyes, and when I open them again, I want to see a real miracle, a big Mac and fries, and don't forget the drink. Ok, I'm closing my eyes now, I'll count to ten, and then I'll open them again. One two three four five six seven eight nine and now ten. I'm opening my eyes now. Well God, where are they, awe never mind, you're just another loser, like everything else in my life. What the hell am I doing talking to myself? Am I losing it, talking to nobody, no one? Maybe I'll become like a crazed lunatic roaming around the bush naked, like big foot, screaming at the top of my lungs, I want a big Mac and fries, I want a big Mac and fries. That's what life has reduced me too, a big Mac and fries. Well, maybe I should try and sleep. If I can only fall asleep, tomorrow will come a little faster. I'm so thirsty, so hungry.

Joe lies on the ground and after a while he falls asleep again. When he awakes he's in darkness again. It is raining hard outside and he hears thunder, lightning streaks across the sky. It is dark in his tent, but he senses someone else sitting inside his tent with him. When the lighting lights up the sky, he thinks he sees the image of a man sitting beside him, he feels for his stick and holds it in his hand.

Joe

Hey, who are you? You better get out. I never invited you in here.

The image doesn't say anything. He just sits there not appearing to be moving.

Joe

Look, this is my tent, if you need a place to stay, you can't stay here. There is only room enough for me in here, you hear me, only me.

The figure of a man still doesn't move.

Joe

Look, I got a large stick in my hand; you don't move from here, I'll beat the crap right out of you. Say something.

Lightning streaks across the sky and Joe gets a better look at the figure.

Joe

You look familiar, I've seen you some where before. Tell me who you are.

The figure finally speaks.

Figure

You know me alright; I'm someone from your past.

Joe

What is your name, tell me your name.

Figure

Frank

Joe

Frank, Frank the farmer, what the heck are you doing here?

Joe stands up and holds the stick towards Frank.

Joe

You know, I almost killed you for what you did to me, you bastard pervert.

Frank

I was drunk; I didn't know what I was doing?

Joe

Don't lie; you just used that as an excuse. You raped me and you enjoyed every moment of it, you just started drinking to give you the courage to take advantage of me, you had it all planned out.

Frank

No, it was all a mistake; I was all blacked out from drinking too much.

Joe

You messed me up big time you bastard, and now you're trying to deny it.

Frank

Honest, you've got to believe me. I would never hurt anybody. I'm not like that.

Joe begins hitting frank with his stick; Frank puts his hands up to protect his head.

Joe

Admit that your bastard. Admit what you fricken did to me.

Frank

No, no, I don't know what you are talking about; you've got the wrong guy.

Joe continues hitting Frank over and over again and begins crying. Frank screams in agonizing pain.JoeLiar, Liar, you're a shit faced liar, you hurt me bad, I'll never forget the pain you put me through, the way you made me feel, your sadistic laugh.

Frank

No, no, please stop, I'm begging you, please stop it.

Joe

Why should I stop? Did you stop when I begged and pleaded with you? When you turned me over and used me like a woman, sent shocking pain through every inch of my body, I begged you, please stop, you're hurting me. Did you stop? No you just kept on until you got what you wanted. I hate you, I hate you.

Frank

No, I'm telling you, it must have been someone else who dragged you into the bedroom that night; you have me confused with someone else.

Joe screams and cries even louder, and grabs the stick with both hands and swings it at Frank with all his might.

Joe

I thought you couldn't remember, you god damn low life piece of trash. Admit it; all I want you to do is admit it.

Franks continues screaming.

Frank

Alright, alright, I admit it, I admit it all.

Joe

Admit what, I want you to say it, say what you did to me.

Frank

I got drunk and raped you, now please stop, please stop. I deserved the beating you gave me, it wasn't your fault.

Joe

Now I'm going to kill you, you bastard.

Joe continues screaming and crying at the top of his lungs. The image of Frank disappears and Joe continues hitting the ground. He screams and cries himself to sleep. Joe wakes up and finds himself in the middle of a red sandy desert. He is all alone; he looks all around himself, makes complete 360 degree turns. He sees nothing but miles and miles of nothing but sand. He starts yelling out.

SCENE 3 Dessert

Joe

Hello, hello, is anyone out there, can anyone hear me? Oh my god, I'm all alone hear. Nothing, no-one in sight. How did I get here? What am I doing here? Hey, is anyone around? If you can hear me, say something. I'm lost; I don't know how I got here. Someone please answer me, anyone. Man now I'm really screwed, I'm scared, and my biggest fear is no-one is ever going to find me, way out here.

Joe drops to his knees and slouches down into the sand. He picks up sand in both of his hands and lets it flow from his hands.

Joe

There's no one here but me and all this stinking rotten sand, miles and miles of worthless sand. Am I dead? What I get myself into?

Joe then looks up and see and old man walking towards him in the distance. There is a sand pit between him and the old man. Joe sees it, but the old man walks towards it as if he doesn't notice it. Joe jumps up and starts running towards the old man, yelling.

Joe

What the hell, where'd you come from? Stop, stop, you're going to fall in; man can't you see the pit?

The old man continues walking towards the pit and starts slipping into it. Joe continues running towards him, still yelling. Joe grabs the old man and pulls him out from the pit and they both fall to the ground. Joe gets up and helps the old man up. He brushes the sand off him.

Joe

Man, didn't you see the pit? What were you thinking? You could have got yourself killed.

The old man looks at Joe, smiles and speaks to him.

Old Man

And by the way, you're from the Bear Clan.

Joe

What, and how do you know that?

Old Man

Cause that's the only animal that came to me, I see you as a Bear.

At that moment Joe wakes up and finds himself lying in the middle of his tent again. He looks outside his tent and takes the two skinny polls and crosses them.

SCENE 4 Pipestone pit to Joe and the Elderly man.

Joe

After that, Lightning came with some of his family members; they brought plenty of food and water. They laid a blanket on the ground and we had a feast. Man, I never thought water could taste so good, and man did I eat.

Elder

Wow, those were some powerful visions you had. How did you feel after that experience?

Joe

I felt great, like I had a different view of my world.

Elder

Did you ever confront him?

Joe

Confront who?

Elder

Frank, the guy who, you know.

Joe

No, I found out a few years later he did the same to another foster kid. The kid told his social worker and Frank got charged and convicted, and was sent to jail for five years. I guess knowing that was enough for me, so I thought.

Elder

I guess.

Joe

You know, I was in many foster homes, not one of them was ever good to me, even the native one. She was a single woman and she had a daughter a few years younger than me.

SCENE 5—Native foster home, Joe and Native foster mom, she is drinking beer. Joe is watching television, sitting on a chair; she is sitting on the couch, with her daughter.

Native foster mom.

Turn that damn TV down, are you deaf of something?

Joe gets up and turns the television down, he then sits down again.

Native foster mom

You know Joe, you're lucky you're living with me. Not to many foster homes that are native you know.

Joe continues looking at the television.

Native foster mom

Are you listening to me Joe?

Joe

Yeah, I'm listening

Native foster mom

I'm telling you, you better thank your lucky stars that there are people like me around to take you in when nobody else wanted you.

Joe fidgets on his chair.

Native foster mom.

Yeah, you're kind of like one of those throw away kids, kids nobody else wants.

Joe

What you talking about, I'm not like that.

Native foster mom

Sure you are, it's a good thing I've got a good heart, to take in someone like you.

Joe

Why you talking to me like that?

Native foster mom

Cause it's true, your here cause nobody else wants you, you're like a nobody's child.

Joe

No I'm not.

Native foster mom

You might as well face the truth now Joe. If it wasn't for people like me, you'd be on the street, begging for nickels and dimes. Your mom and your dad didn't want you, they just threw you away, like an old piece of furniture.

Joe

You don't know that, you don't know anything about my mom and dad, you know shit.

Native foster mom pulls her daughter close to her and gives her hug, as if she just wants to taunt Joe.

Native foster mom

Yeah, then where are they? Me, I been taking care of my little girl since she was born. Your mom and dad just had you, and couldn't wait to push you out the door.

Joe just put his head down and stares deep into the television set, he had and angry and distant look in his eyes.

Foster sister.

Mom, are we going to get my Indian name tomorrow, like you promised.

Native foster mom

Sure we are, we're heading out to the reserve first thing in the morning, your uncles picking us up.

Foster sister

What about Joe, is he coming to?

Native foster mom

No, why should we take him for, you know the sweat lodge is a sacred place. Kids like Joe, can't come around places like that.

Foster sister

Maybe he can come and get an Indian name too.

Native foster mom

He already has Indian name, I gave him one already, "Throw Away Child".

The foster mom and daughter both look towards Joe and chuckle. Joe clenches his fist keeping his head down.

SCENE—6 pipe stone pit with Joe and the Elder

Joe

You know, the next day they went out to their reservation and came back later that evening. My foster sister got her name and my native foster mom threw a big party for her. Man, it was like a big birthday party with balloons, hotdogs and lots of cake and ice cream. I was so jealous. I wanted to have a big party thrown for me too.

Elder

So what did you do?

Joe

Well, at the time I was going to this aboriginal school in Winnipeg. I heard they were going to take anybody that wanted to go to East Selkirk, which is only about a thirty minute ride from Winnipeg. I really wanted to have an Indian name and really believed my foster mom would also throw a party for me too; I don't know why I even thought that.

Elder

So what happened?

Joe

Well, I signed up and went to the sweat. I passed my tobacco and the guy running the sweat gave me my name. I was so excited. When I got back to the city, I ran home to tell my foster mom.

SCENE—7 Native Foster mom's living room, she's drinking beer again.

Joe

Guess what?

Native foster mom

You been suspended from school again.

Joe

No, I went to a sweat

Native foster mom

With who?

Joe

My school.

Native foster mom

What kind of school are they running over there anyway? They should be teaching you kids, important stuff like reading and writing, not wasting your time taking you to sweats. No wonder you can't effin read.

Joe

I got my Indian name too.

Native foster mom.

So, why you telling me for, as if I care, probably don't mean nothing anyway.

Joe

You want to know what it is.

Native foster mom
Let me guess, is it, mmm, "Throw Away child"

Native foster mom chuckles to herself.

Joe

No, My Indian name is," Black Eagle Thunderbird Man".

Native foster mom

What did you say?

Joe

My Indian name is, "Black Eagle Thunderbird Man".

Native foster mom

You can't have a name like that. Who-ever gave you that name, didn't know what the hell he was doing. Probably some fake medicine man, trying to make a name for himself.

Joe

Why you putting my name down for? Why you always putting me down?

Native foster mom

Cause you're an effin disrespectful, smart ass, dumb asshole kid.

Joe

Are you going to throw me a party too?

Native foster mom

A party, why the hell should I throw a party for you?

Joe

Because, I got my Indian name, that's why.

Native foster mom

You don't effin deserve anything.

The native foster mom pulls off her shoe and runs up to Joe and starts hitting him with it.

Native foster mom

Why you little bastard, you don't deserve that name either.

Joe

What did I do? Why are you hitting me for? I ain't done nothing wrong.

Native foster mom

That was my dead grandfather's name. He was a great medicine man. That can't be your name. A loser like you can't have a name like that, you're just a loser kid, I hate you.

Joe

Why, what the hell is wrong with you?

Joe runs out the door.

Native foster mom

Yeah, that's right, run you little bastard, and don't you ever come back, you hear me, don't you ever show your sorry ass; throw away face, around here again.

SCENE—8 pipestone pit

Joe

I slept in the park that night feeling so hurt and confused, wishing I had someone anyone I could turn too, but as usual, I had no one. When I got home the next day she took me to the child and family agency and just dropped me off. Just like that, like I was a nothing, and I really felt like a nothing too.

Elder

Wow that sounds like some really messed up lady.

Joe

Yeah, she sure was. I thought because she was a native woman, maybe she would understand where I was coming from; instead, she made me feel even worse.

Elder

Well, you got to understand; a lot of our people have been really damaged, and haven't done any healing.

Joe

Well, I guess I thought, because she was into the culture, you know going to sweats and stuff that she would be all right.

Elder

You know, a lot of people just jump into the culture without doing any healing. They bring their messed up thinking and messed up views and mesh it with traditional stuff, it doesn't work that way.

Joe

What do you mean?

Elder

Well, it's like this, if you grow up in an alcoholic home, you learn alcoholic beliefs and values, alcoholic ways of doing stuff. Like when I grew up, in my alcoholic home, I learned three rules, don't talk, don't trust, and don't feel. I had to learn to break those rules, in order to free myself from my destructive lifestyle and behaviour.

Joe

But it's so much work.

Elder

Yeah, but it's worth it in the end. You know it's kind of like leaving an abusive relationship. You can run half way across the country to get away from it, the trouble is, you have to bring yourself with you, and you bring your baggage with you and recreate the same kind of relationship you left behind.

Joe

Yeah, I think I know what you mean; I've done that more than a few times myself.

Elder
You when you try and mix alcoholic values with traditional values, it becomes something completely different, sure on the outside it may look like it, but on the inside is where you find the garbage you've stashed.

Joe

You know, that makes a lot of sense, that kind of reminds me of a time I went to a sweat lodge and while I was in there, it was pitch-black dark, I couldn't see anything, the guy conducting it was sitting next to me and I swear he was trying to feel me up.

SCENE—9 trail in bush leading away from a sweat lodge with the lodge conductor

Joe

I need to talk to you.

Lodge conductor

Yeah, about what?

Joe

Why were you trying to touch me?

Lodge conductor

What you talking about?

Joe

You know what I'm talking about, trying to feel me up.

Lodge conductor

I was only trying to doctor you; I can't doctor you without touching you. It's the only way it works, traditionally our people very affectionate, we did a lot of touching, that's in our culture.

Joe

But I didn't ask you to do anything to me; I didn't ask to be doctored.

Lodge conductor

Well, then why did you come here, in the first place?

Joe

I came to pray, for healing.

Lodge conductor

So, all I did was try to heal you, with my hands, that's how I do it.

Joe

I think you tried to do more than just heal me. I think you were trying to get your jollies from trying to touch me. There's nothing wrong with me down there.

Lodge conductor

How dare you, talking to me like that, you certainly have your nerve. You know, maybe before you come to another sweat lodge, you should learn to have a little more respect for your elders. You don't talk to your elders that way.

Joe

Well, I'm been told, respect is something you earn, first from respecting yourself.

Lodge conductor

No, you must first learn to respect your elders, don't question things you don't understand, you can't question my authority.

Joe

Well, how in the hell am I suppose to understand stuff, If I can't ask questions, it makes no sense.

Lodge conductor

Well, that's the way it is, you young people, trouble with you is, you don't know how to listen.

Joe

Well, I don't think an elder should be using the sweat lodge to try and feel people up in. How can I have respect for someone that does that?

Lodge conductor

You know, I doctor people from all over the world, I am respected by everybody. Anyway, why should a little playful touching bother you, from what I understand, you made a living by letting old men touch you all the time.

Joe

What I did in the past, is where I'd like to leave it, in the past. That's exactly the reason I came here today, to heal from my past, not to have it thrown in my face.

Lodge conductor

Well, talk is, I here you enjoyed it.

Joe

You think I enjoyed it? Well you know what? I hated it, and I still hate it. And that still doesn't give you the right to touch me in places I don't want to be touched. Nobody can touch me without my permission.

Lodge conductor

Look, I have children and a wife that I love very much, I don't need to mess around with a hustling faggot like you, thinking that everyone is always trying to get into your pants. Get the hell out of here and I don't want to ever see you here again until you learn to have respect for your elders.

Joe

Why is it, when I try and stand up for myself, because I think I'm being taken advantage of, people like you choose to hid behind all that cultural stuff, and try and make me think that I've done something wrong. That's bullshit.

Lodge conductor

This is scared ground, you watch your mouth, when you come here, or the grandfathers will string you alive. Don't you ever come here with that kind of attitude again?

Joe

Don't worry, this is the last sweat lodge, I'll ever come to for the rest of my life.

Joe walks away angry and upset, he turns back to the Lodge conductor and gives him the middle finger.

SCENE—10 back in the pipestone pit.

Joe

I was as so mad at him; I wanted to pick a stick off the ground and run back and beat the shit right out of him.

Elder

Well, some people want to be instant medicine people, just like having instant coffee; it takes years to do this job. How can they help others deal with their addictions, when they haven't even dealt with their own?

Joe

Yeah, it doesn't make sense, some even leave there wife's and children for young girls, after they've gained a little bit of status and recognition. Some have even turned it into a business to make enough money to feed the slot machines at the casinos every night.

Elder

Well, thank God we're not all like that, you can't paint us all with the same brush. You know, they say that no sweat lodge is an evil one, like there no such thing as bad medicine, only people doing bad things with good medicine.

Joe

Yeah, I know, it took me a long time to get over what happened to me that day. But eventually I went to other sweats, but not one run by him. People must be pretty desperate to follow him.

Elder

Well, sometimes as human beings, we all want to feel we belong and in our need, we refuse to see when we are being taken advantage of.

Joe

Well, I really think that can be dangerous, it's supposed to be a place where our people can get healing. Not to be victimized all over again. It makes the healing that much more difficult, when you don't know who you can trust.

Elder

Yeah, but you got to trust someone.

Joe

Yeah I guess, but it becomes even harder when everywhere you turn, you feel someone is out to get you. Like the time I was living on the streets, I thought I was safe when I was amongst my own people. One night I was walking around late at night, when a group of young native boys approached me.

SCENE—11 Street in downtown Winnipeg, its late at night. Joe is approached by a group of five young native boys. The leader looked like he had a scar on the side of his mouth.

Scar face

Hey man, you got a smoke?

Joe

No, sorry man, I ain't got nothing.

Scar face

What about money, got any money?

Joe

No man, I'm poor, ain't got nothing.

Scar face

Come on man, you must have some coin, are you trying to hold out on us?

Joe digs in his pockets and pulls them inside out.

Joe

Told you man, I ain't got anything, not a dime to my name.

Joe tries to ignore the five youth and tries to brush past them. Scar face punches Joe in the back of the head. Joe grabs the back of his head and looks at Scar face.

Joe

Hey man, what the hell you do that for? I'm just trying to go home, don't want no trouble.

Scar face

Well, don't fricken walk away when I'm talking to you! Nobody fricken walks away from me when I'm talking to them. Who you down with?

Joe

What do you mean?

Scar face

What, are you stupid? Who you running with, what gang are you in?

Joe

I'm with nobody, no gang.

Scar face

Why you wearing that red cap for?

Joe

Was given to me by a friend of mine?

Scar face

What friend, don't see no friend around.

Joe

That's cause he's dead, hung himself.

Scar face

That so sad, oh boo who. So I guess, since he's dead, he won't mind if I keep the cap.

Scar face grabs the cap from Joe's head. Joe tries to get it back.

Joe

No, give me that, it's all I've got left of my friend Thomas. Please give it back to me.

Scar face

Are you trying to tell me what to do? I hate people who try and tell me what to do. Nobody tells me what to do.

Joe

Please, I need that cap.

Scar face slaps Joe across the face and makes his mouth bleed. Joe wipes the blood mouth.

Scar face

Do I need to teach you respect boy?

Joe

Why you doing this to me? I ain't done nothing to you, I'm a nobody, I've got nothing.

Scar face

Well, you're on my turf, the street belongs to me.

Joe

What the hell do you mean, it's a free country, I thought the street belongs to everyone.

Scar face

Yeah, well you thought wrong.
Scar face slaps Joe again across the face, this time knocking him to the ground.

Joe

Why don't you just leave me alone? I ain't bothering no-one, wasn't bothering you. I was just minding my own business.

At that point Scar face kicks him in the face. Joe jumps up and runs after Scar face and head butts him in the stomach. Scar face falls to the ground and Joe starts punching Scar face in the face. Scar face yells to his buddies.

Scar face

Get him.

One of the other big boys kicks Joe in the rib cage and Joe falls to the side off of Scar face. Everyone then jumps on Joe and begin kicking and punching him on the head and then they start stomping him all over the rest of his body for a few minutes. They all stop and back off Joe. Joe lays on the ground unconscious. One of the other youth says.

Second youth

Doesn't look like he's breathing, I think we killed him.

Scar face

Good for the fucker, teach him to try and mess with me. Nobody tries and messes with me and lives.

Second Youth

Well, we can't just leave him here. The cops will be all over the place.

Scar face grabs Joe by the feet and looks at the others.

Scar face

Well, you heard him, don't just stand there, help me drag him into the back lane, we'll throw his body into a dumpster back there; we'll let the garbage men do the rest. They never check them before they dump them got rid of a bitch that way.

All five youth drag Joe to the lane and throw him into a dumpster. They then all take off running into the darkness.

SCENE—12 Pipestone pit

Joe

You know, I regained consciousness inside that dumpster. My head hurt like hell and I felt like they had broken every bone in my body. I thought for sure I was going to die.

Elder

Wow, so what did you do?

Joe

I lay there crying for a couple of hours thinking for sure I was going to die. I then I tried to help myself out of the dumpster. I had a hard time breathing; I think I had a few broken ribs. I couldn't climb out, no matter what I did; I was in way too much pain. I think I fell asleep for a while.

Elder

Wow, that really must have been one scary time.

Joe

Yeah, it sure was, I didn't really want to make any noise because I was afraid those boys might come back and finish the job.

Elder

So how did you manage to get out?

Joe

Well, later on that day, an older man by the name of Daniel was throwing out his trash and when he opened the lid, he saw me lying inside. I think the sight of me scared the shit right out of him, because he closed the lid quickly and then came back again to have a second look.

SCENE—13 Dumpster in back lane.

Daniel

Hey are you alright?

Joe

I don't know. Can you help me get out?

Daniel

You know, I'll go get some help, I'll call the cops, get you an ambulance.

Joe

No, please, no cops. I'll be ok; I just need a little help.

Daniel

I think you need more than a little help; you need to be in a hospital. Come on; let me at least call you an ambulance.

Joe

No, they'll call the cops, and I can't stand cops. Come on, at least try and help me out of here.

Daniel

Ok, I'll try, but if I can't help you out, I going to have to call someone.

Daniel reaches inside and tries to help Joe out of the dumpster. Joe screams from the pain of being moved. Daniel lets go.

Daniel

Please let me call some, get you some help. You're in pretty bad shape.

Joe

No, just try one more time, once I get out of here, I'll be ok. Think you could find something to bite on, a stick or something. I saw someone in an old western move bite on a stick to help with the pain.

Daniel looks around and then comes back with a stick; he places it into Joe's mouth and looks around. He saw another younger man walk by. He calls to the younger man.

Daniel

Hey, you, can you come and give me a hand here.

The younger man walks up to the dumpster and looks inside.

Younger man

Holy shit, you got to get this guy to a hospital.

Daniel

No, he doesn't want to go there, he just wants help to get out.

Younger man

Well, I try.

Joe bites down hard on the stick and the two men together help Joe out of the dumpster and sits Joe on an old armchair beside it.

Joe

Guys, I really appreciate this.

Younger man

We'll you take care of yourself, I've got to go or I'll be late for work.

Daniel

Yeah, thanks a lot mister, I don't think I could have done it on my own

Younger man

No, makes sure he gets some help.

Daniel

I will.

Daniel shakes the younger man's hand and the younger man walks away. Daniel then turns his attention back to Joe.

Daniel

So now what are you going to do?

Joe

Oh, just leave me here, I'll be ok now. Thanks.

Daniel

I can't just leave you here, let me at least call someone from your family to come and get you. You got a number?

Joe

Uh, I got no one, no family. Don't make me laugh; it hurts too much, in more ways than you know.

Daniel

Well, at least let me help you get home, where do you live?

Joe

Got no home either, Like I said, just leave me here, I'll be ok, you've done enough for me. Thanks.

Daniel

You know, I live in this apartment block right behind this dumpster, I have a suite, you can stay on my couch for a few days, until you get on your feet again.

Joe

No thanks, don't want to put you out or anything. And why would you do that anyway, I'm nobody to you, why waste your time, for all you know, I could be some serial killer who will kill you in your sleep, in the middle of the night. Or maybe you want me for other reasons. One thing I've learned, nobody does you something for nothing.

Daniel

You know, I'm an old man, probably not going to be around this earth much longer. Never been married, got no kids. At my age, all I do is live day to day. I feel the need to do something good before I go to meet my maker, and besides, it gets lonely living all alone, could certainly use the company. I believe if you do something good to help someone that goodness will somehow come back to you.

Joe

Really, Ok thanks, I guess I really don't have much choice, do I?

Daniel

No sir, I don't think you do. But I'm warning you, if you don't get any better, or you get any worse, I'm calling you an ambulance, you hear, and I won't take no for an answer.

Joe

I hear, ok, that's a deal.

SCENE—14 Pipestone pit.

Joe

You know, before that night, when those boys beat me up, I thought everything that could be taken from me had already been taken. But those five youth took something even deeper than that. It's really hard to explain what they took from me. It was like they seemed to reach deep down into the pit of my soul and they managed to grab something out, and it hurt more than any other beating anyone else could have given me. What even made it so much more difficult for me to understand was, they were my people, our youth. How could someone carry so much hate in their hearts that they can just beat up some, for no reason, and just leave them there to die, with no remorse any regret. It doesn't make any sense. And the cap Thomas gave me wasn't just any cap.

Elder

Sometimes that's the way things are, just senseless. You know, you could drive yourself crazy, trying to find an answer, when really, there isn't one.

Joe

I walked around in fear for a long time after that, whenever I would see a young native person, I would run as fast as I can, thinking the worst of them.

Elder

Yeah, but they're not all like that you know, many have really good kind hearts.

Joe

You know, I kept thinking of what Scar face said, he had to teach me respect. How could I respect someone like him, all he did was cause me to fear him, not respect him. And I had such a difficult time shaking that overwhelming fear. I wanted to kill the fear, kill him, and kill everyone who resembled him.

Elder

Yes, that's funny how many young people think getting someone to fear you, is somehow a form of respect. We as human beings, don't like to have the emotion of fear in us, we automatically want to kill it. Like those old movies I used to watch, the minute any common people fear anything, they grab, sticks pitchforks, guns and knives and try to kill something on order not to feel fear. It's no wonder why, in the paper you read about young people in street gangs get killed almost every day.

Joe

But the good that came out of that night was me meeting Daniel. At first though I really didn't trust him, thought for sure he was going to ask me for favors, you know, sexual. But instead that old man took care of me like nobody else ever did. It sure felt good for someone to take care of me, the way he did. I couldn't eat any solid foods for a while, se he fed me some chicken and tomato soup for the first couple of days. Man, I was in so much pain, he even got me some pain killers to take which helped me sleep a little better.

Elder

Sounds like a person with real heart.

Joe

Yeah, he even got me some really good used clothes. He would fill up his bathtub and help me get in and out. It was the best feeling of my life, lying there in that tub of soothing warm water, the feeling of having fresh clean clothes touching your body after a relaxing bath.

Elder

Wow.

Joe

Yeah, somehow he made me feel like a human being, for the first time in my life. And the weird part was, I felt real guilty taking Daniels help, the old man's kindness. It was as if I didn't deserve it or something, or I owed him something and he would anytime ask me for something in exchange.

Elder

And did he?

Joe

No, nothing, not ever. It was as if his payment was doing things for me, the better I got, the happier he became. I could see it in his eyes, his face, and his smile, like I gave him a purpose, a reason to live.

Elder

Yeah, poor people used to be like that, getting pleasure out of helping people. Like my grandmother, when people came to visit her, she would automatically set the table and feed them. They didn't have to say thank you, they could see it, like you said, in her eyes, her face and smile. And when her visitors left, she always said to them, Meegwetch ka-beshan ohma, giwabamin.

Joe

What does that mean?

Elder

It's Ojibway, It means, thank you for coming to my place to visit and see me, to come see me.

Joe

Wow, that's powerful.

Elder

Why didn't you go to a hospital?

Joe

Are you kidding? Once I went to the emergency in a hospital in Winnipeg. Man, they treat animals better in the zoo. The nurses are so cold and uncaring. I got the impression, they couldn't care less of you lived or died, and they especially ignored you if you were an Indian. Lots of people came and left without even getting treatment, the wait was too long. I heard one guy came in a waited over 34 hours to see a doctor. They said he died there in his wheelchair. He was dead for a few hours and the whole fricken hospital didn't even notice. Another patient had to go tell them. You know, they have all these big modern buildings, spend millions of dollars on research and health care, and our people are sicker than ever.

Elder

That's right hey.

Joe

You know, I think there is some sort of conspiracy out there to keep us from getting better. Can you imagine how many white people would be out of a job if all our illnesses were cured? How many nurses and doctors would be out of a job? And the jails, the lawyers, the judges, the prosecutors, the guards the police, they'd all be out of work if our people stopped getting in trouble with the law. I think the whole economy would collapse. Wouldn't that be funny?

Elder

Yeah, come to think of it, it would. So, what ever happened to the old man Daniel?

Joe, smiles.

Joe

Well, it took me about a month for my body to heal, and he let me stay with him and help me find place of my own. He still stays at the same place; I pop in on him every now and then, just to see how he's doing.

Elder

Wow, you got lucky; people like Daniel are a rare find.

Joe

And you know what else? He asked me one day if I ever had a grandfather. I told him no, don't know what having a grandfather feels like. He told me, well you have one know if you want one. So I guess you could say, I adopted Daniel as my grandfather, and he adopted me as his grandson. So now when I see him I call him grandfather.

Elder

You know, that how it used to work with our people. When a child became orphaned for what even reason, there was no question about whose responsibility it was to take care of him or her. Someone in the community automatically took them in, even if they knew they wouldn't be getting paid to keep them. Nowadays, it's all about money, and how much money.

Joe

Yeah, I was in the system, and it's true, it seems like to me it's all about the money. It's funny how money changes some people.

Elder

Yeah, even one weekend, I was on my way to a Sundance in a reserve near Winnipeg. One of my son's friends came over and I started talking to him. He said he was living in a foster home because his mother had a crack addiction. He found out the Sundance I was going to was being held in the same reserve he was from. He said he had a grandmother living there and he wanted to see her. He asked me if he could hitch a ride there so he could spend the weekend with her. I asked if what his foster parents would say if he were to leave the city for the weekend. He told me, they don't care, I don't even live there, I only go there every two weeks to get my allowance.

Joe

So did you take him?

Elder

Yeah, I dropped him off at his grandmother's house and told him, I would pick him back up on Sunday, after the Sundance. When the Sundance ended, I went looking him all over the reserve, but he was nowhere to be found.

Joe

So what did you do?

Elder

There was nothing I could do, I just went back home to Winnipeg. When I got home he was in my yard, playing ball in with my son. So I went up to him and asked him how he got back to the city. He had this really hurt look in his eyes. He said, as soon as he walked into his grandmother's house, she looked at him, walked straight to the telephone and called his social worker. She said to his social worker, why is he here? I'm not getting paid to keep him. He said, not long afterward, his social worker showed up and he was on his way back to Winnipeg.

Joe

Man, his own flesh and blood grandmother did that to him.

Elder

Afraid so, he later told me that his grandmother played favorites, he went on to say, but I don't care. But, I could tell, deep down inside it did bother him.

Joe

Well, I guess, I think stuff like that would bother anybody. That's probably why so many of our youth are so messed up, why they are so full of hate and resentment, maybe why I got beaten up, because they were mad at someone else, and I just happened to in the wrong place at the wrong time. It really had nothing to do with me.

Elder

Afraid so, you know, now-a-days, there is so much disconnection between our youth and elders, the gap is so wide, even to me, and it is sometimes overwhelming.

Joe

That's so sad, and I thought I was the only one.

Joe and the elder continue trying to chip away chunks of the rock.

Joe

Hey, do you believe in ghosts?

Elder

Well yea, the grandmothers and grandfathers come into the sweat lodges all the time.

Joe

No, not like that, like the kind that looks like a real person, but disappear and you never see them again, or they appear and disappear.

Elder

Well, I guess in the spirit world, anything is possible, although personally, I've never seen something like that myself. Why do you ask?

Joe

Well, a few months after I tried hanging myself, I was trying to get my life back on track. My boss gave me another chance, gave me back my roofing job, I even took some classes to learn to read, hey, I even got my driver's license. My boss was so impressed with me that he would let me take the company truck home on the weekends. Anyway, one Friday night, for some reason or another, I was feeling very depressed, well I guess, I was thinking about it for a long time. I was going to hang myself again. This time I thought, I would do it right. I bought a rope and that evening I was really going to do myself in.

Elder

Yeah, and so, what happened?

SCENE—15 Joe's apartment

Joe

Well, I decided I was going to go outside and smoke my last smoke on the front steps of the building I was living in. While I was having my smoke and contemplating suicide, a young native guy walked by, well this was after those boys gave me a beating, and normally I didn't want anything to do with them, but at the time I thought, what the hell, I was going to die anyway, so I guess I didn't care. I was thinking, you can kill me if you want, save me the trouble. His name was John and I noticed he was carrying a newspaper.

John

Hey man, you got any wheels?

Joe

No, not my own, I only got my boss's truck. Why?

John

Well, I want to get myself a dog, there's one in the newspaper, but its way out on the outskirts of the city, I really have no way of getting there. You think you could give me a ride?

Joe

No, I'm kind of busy; I've got something I have to do. You'll have to find someone else.

John

Well, I've asked everyone I know with wheels, they all say the same thing; they have something else to do. It won't take long.

Joe

Sorry man, like I said, I have something else to do.

John

Come on man, I really want this dog; I won't ever ask you for anything again. Please, once I get my dog, you can do whatever it is you need to do later.

SCENE—16 Joe back in the pipestone pit.

Joe

You know, I thought about it for while, and then I thought to myself, well, I do my last good deed before I kill myself, I guess another hour or two won't really make a difference.

Joe, back on his front steps.

Joe

Ok then man, I'll help you get your stinking dog, but after that you promise to leave me alone, I got something I really need to do.

John

Gee thanks man.

Joe and John get into the truck and drive way out near the out skirts of the city. They went and knocked on the door and a large man let us in and led us to a room with about eight young pups. John picks up each pup and examined them all one by one.

Joe

Ok man, pick one and let's get out of here. Why you taking so long?

John

Wait, I want to make sure I get just the right one.

Joe

Well, they all look the same to me, dogs a dog.

John looks at one of the dogs and turns to Joe.

John

Well, I kind of like this one, but. I don't know, it's not quite what I was looking for.

Joe

What do you mean?

John

Well, none of these dogs are what I really wanted, sorry.

Joe shakes his head.

Joe

Well, let's get out of here then.

John and Joe leave that house and head back to the north end; they stopped at a doughnut place and had a doughnut and a coffee. They then went back to Joe's place and end up sitting in his living room.

John

You mind if I have a smoke in here.

Joe

Sure, I smoke, or didn't you notice.

John

No, I don't mean that kind of smoke, I mean smoke a joint.

Joe

Sure, why not, in a little while it won't make a difference anyway, nothing's going to make a difference.

John

What do you mean?

Joe

Oh, nothing. Hurry up, smoke it and go, there's something I need to do.

John takes out his wallet and pulls out a piece of tin foil with weed in it. He takes some rolling papers from his back pocket and rolls himself a joint. He then lights it up and takes a few deep and lasting drags. A small picture of a little girls falls from his wallet to the floor. Joe picks it up and hands it to John.

Joe

You dropped something.

John

It's a picture of my little girl. She beautiful, don't you think. Do you have any kids?

Joe

Almost,

John

What do you mean almost?

Joe

What's with all the questions?

John

Just asking, making conversation.

Joe

Had a little girl, she died at birth.

John

Sorry, me my little girl lives in Ontario, with her mom, left me for my so called best friend. I miss my daughter so much.

Joe

So, why don't you go and see her then?

John

I wish I could, my ex would have me arrested. She said if I come around, she would tell the police I abused her, and she'll have me thrown in jail.

Joe

She can't do that with any proof.

John

Damn rights she can, they have this new law now, zero tolerance, they always believe whatever the woman says, and the guy ends up in the slammer.

Joe

That's fucked up man.

John

Tell me about it. You know, a friend of mine's ex called him one day out of the blue. They had four kids together before he caught her in bed with his brother. They had a big fight and he went to jail for a while. Well, anyway, she calls him up and tells him the kids miss him. They want him to come and see them. He tells his ex, what about the restraining order you have against me. She tells him, oh don't worry about that, I won't say nothing if you won't.

Joe

So did he go and see his kids?

John

On yeah, he spent whole evening with them. After that, she asked him to spend the night; you know to be there for his kids in the morning. She made a bed for him on the sofa. Next thing he knows he's being awaken by two big city cops. They handcuff him and lead him out the front door. As they take him out, she walks near him and whispers in his ear, if I can't have you, nobody else will. They took him straight to jail.

Joe

Man, that sucks, that really sucks. Anyway, you've got to go, it's already after midnight.

John

Hey, you know what, Tomorrow's Saturday.

Joe

So, big deal, tomorrows Saturday, just another day to me.

John

Well, Saturday always has the biggest newspaper. I bet there will be lots of dogs in the newspaper tomorrow. Can I come back tomorrow?

Joe

No, forget about it, I'm not driving you around tomorrow, so you could look for a stupid dog. Besides, I told you more than once, I've got something I need to do.

John

Well, I'll come first thing in the morning, we'll get a dog quick, and then you'll have plenty of time to do whatever you need to do.

Joe

Are you nuts, I said no, are you hard of hearing?

John

Look man, I'll be quick choosing a dog this time, please; I really have to have a dog.

Joe thinks about it again and decides that he should at least do this last good deed of his life. He still will have plenty of time after he helps John get his dog.

Joe

Ok, you can come back first thing in the morning, but make sure you're here bright and early.

John

Thanks, I'll be here first thing.

John left and Joe went to sleep, next thing he remembers, there was someone banging on his door. He gets up and answered the door and there is John, bright and early with the thickest Saturday newspaper he ever saw. Joe invites him in and makes some coffee.

John

See, I told you there would be lots of dogs in the Saturday newspaper.

Joe

You don't expect me to drive you to every single one of those places do you?

John

Well, no, but we can go to as many as we have time for. We'll start with the ones that are close.

Joe

Did you have breakfast yet?

John

No, never had anything to eat since that doughnut you bought me last night. I was so excited about getting a dog today; I guess I forgot to eat anything.

Joe

Well, I'll cook us up a quick breakfast before we go. You like bacon and eggs?

John

For sure, I'd love some.

Joe

Bacon and eggs; coming up. Listen, why are you so bent on getting a dog anyway?

John

Well, after I my ex left me, I got really lonely; I even tried to kill myself. I took two different kinds of pills. I thought I would just go to sleep and die, but instead, I was in a whole lot of pain. My neighbours heard me yelling and called the cops. I was rushed to the hospital and had my stomach pumped. The doctor said I was lucky I took both bottles; they were somehow battling each other in my stomach. Anyway, I been going to therapy and they suggested I get myself a dog, you know, to keep me company.

Joe

You think a dog is going to replace your ex-girlfriend.

John

Well, at least it won't be so ugly.

John and Joe both have a good laugh. Joe and John drove around that whole day trying to find just the right dog. Joe actually had a good time going all over the city. John telling me stories of stuff that happened to him or people he knows. They went to every place listed in that newspaper and John still hadn't found the kind of dog he was looking for. Again they ended up at that same doughnut shop and then back at Joe's place, no dog.

SCENE—17 Joe's apartment

Joe

Hey man, I really don't know what kind of dog you want. We wasted the whole day looking at hundreds of dogs and still nothing.

John

Well, the kind of dog I want is, I really don't know what kind, I have this feeling that when I see the one I want, for some reason, I'll know it.

Joe

You know what I think?

John

What Joe?

Joe

I think you must be crazy or something.

John

I'm not crazy, maybe a little slow, but certainly not crazy.

Joe

Or, you really don't want a dog; you just used that as an excuse to get me to drive you all over the fricken city. You probably just wanted to go driving around.

John

Honest Joe, I really do want a dog, just got to find the right one.

Joe

Or, maybe you're trying to find a dog that looks like your ex-girlfriend.

Joe laughs out loud.

John

Funny, it's so funny, I forgot to laugh.

Joe

Well, I guess from now on, you're on your own.

John

What do you mean?

Joe

Well, I've done my good deed, driving you all over the place. You'll have to find someone else to drive you around to get you your mutt.

John

Well, I was kind of hoping that maybe.

Joe

Maybe what?

John

That maybe, I could come back tomorrow.

Joe

Now I know you're crazy. I'm been putting off something I need to do, just for you and your need for a stupid dog, and now, you want me to put it off even longer.

John

Come on, the Sunday paper is always a small one, it won't take long, I'm sure there will only be a few ads for dogs.

Joe

Are you nuts? Forget it.

John

Anyway, what you need to do that's so important?

Joe

That's none of your damn business.

John

OK, then how long do you think what you need to do is going to take?

Joe

I don't know, maybe five, ten minutes tops.

John

Man, is that all, I thought you had something to do that took at least a few hours.

Joe

Well, what I have to do is important, so you have to go now.

John

Well, for me, getting a dog is also important. Listen, if your important stuff is only going to take you a few minutes, you have plenty of time tomorrow, after I get my dog that is.

Joe

Man, what's with you anyway, why can't you take no for an answer.

John

Does that mean you'll do it?

Joe

Yeah, I'll help you get your stinking dog, but this will be the last and final time. If you don't find the mutt you're looking for, then you'll just have to learn to live without one.

John

Last time, I promise.

John leaves Joe's place again and Joe goes to bed. Just as he was snoozing nicely, there was a pounding at the door again. Joe opens the door and there stands John, smiling holding the Sunday paper.

Joe

Man, didn't you go home and sleep?

John

You said bright and early.

Joe

That was for yesterday, I was planning to sleep in a little today, I always try to sleep in on Sundays, and so I won't be tired for work on Monday.

John

Oh, sorry. You want me to go and come back later.

Joe

No, I'm already up now, might as well get this over and done with, the sooner, the better, and I suppose you didn't have breakfast yet either.

John

Nope.

Joe fixes John and himself some breakfast and then they get into the truck and drive off. They go to a few new places until at last they come to a place that had pups John likes. They were a cross between German Sheppard and Border collie. The dog owner led them into his garage where he kept them.

SCENE—18 garage.

John

Man, these are really nice pups.

Joe

See anything you like.

John

I like all of them; I wish I could have all of them.

Joe

Finally; a dog that he likes. So pick one and let's get out of here.

John

Wait, don't rush me, I'm having such a hard time to decide.

John examined each dog very slowly and he finally holds one up.

Joe

Come on, It's getting late.

John

Ok, I think I'll take this one.

Dog Owner

That will be 40 bucks please.

John gives Joe a funny stare.

Joe

You mean you don't have any money, you made me drive you around all bloody weekend, wasting my time and you don't have a penny to your name.

John holding the dog puts his head down and looks towards the ground. Joe digs into his back pocket and pulls out his wallet, takes out $40.00 and hands it to the dog owner.

Joe

Ok now, take your dumb dog and let's get out of here.

John smiles a happy smile.

John

Thank you Joe, I really appreciate this, thanks a million. I'll pay you back someday, I promise.

Joe

Yeah, whatever.

SCENE—19 Pipestone pit

Joe

You know, I never saw John again after that day. He said he lived in a house in the next block, but he never came around again.

Elder

Really, that does seem kind of strange.

Joe

Yeah, I sometimes would drive up and down the streets in the north end, but there was no John in sight. I even drove up and down the back lanes hoping to find John's dog maybe tied up in the backyard, but I couldn't find the dog either.

Elder

Yeah, that is really strange.

Joe

You know, after I went back home and John left, I didn't feel like killing myself anymore. I felt a little better after helping John out. I think he was somehow sent to become a part of my life, at a time when I really needed someone, keep me occupied, take my mind off trying to commit suicide.

Elder

Yeah, it sure seems that way.

Joe

You think he may have been my guardian angel or something.

Elder

You never know, strange unexplainable things happen sometimes.

Joe

I was thinking, maybe he was Jesus himself, or maybe John the Baptist.

Elder

Well, I think that's highly unlikely, They say Jesus drank wine, but I don't think he'd show up smoking a joint, then again, I don't know everything.

Joe and the Elder continue trying to break the rock.

Joe

Man, I'm really getting sick of this. I'm hot, I'm tired and still, no pipestone in sight.

Elder

Oh it's there alright; we just have to go deeper.

Joe

Any deeper and we'll end up in China. Man, what I'd give for a Jackhammer right now. I bet we would get to the pipestone in no time.

Elder

Well, they don't allow Jackhammers, so stop fighting it.

Joe

Why not, I'm sure if there was gold under all this rock, the government would have all kinds of power tools here, big machines, and dynamite.

Elder

No doubt.

Joe

You know, we should just become like them, assimilate ourselves into white society and forget about being Indian.

Elder

Believe me, I've tried that, didn't work for me.

Joe puts his hands up into the sky and looks up.

Joe

To be Indian or not to be Indian, that is the question. You know, if only I could have done something else with my life.

Elder

Like what?

Joe

I don't know, maybe become a singer, or maybe become an actor, you know like that native guy in Hollywood that does all those movies. I think his name is Adam, Adam, something.

Elder

You mean, Adam Beach?

Joe

Yeah, that's the guy. I bet he's got it made, living the life and all. He doesn't have come here and bust rock all day.

Elder

Well, from what I've heard, he's also had a rough life. His mother was killed by a drunk driver and his father drowned six weeks later.

Joe

Really?

Elder

As a matter of fact, he was here last summer digging for pipestone for his pipe, in this very pit we're in right now.

Joe

No way, I can't believe that. If I was him, I'd hire some people to come and chip away at this rock for me.

Elder

What would be the point in that? When things are given to you and you don't really earn it, it's hardly the same thing.

Joe

Yeah, I guess.

Joe and the elder continue chipping away at the rock.

Elder

You know, when we grow up in a dysfunctional family, especially one where there is a lot of abuse. We become cold and hard, just like this rock we're trying to chip away at. We do this in order to survive. We live in a state of denial; our realities become too painful, so we kind of begin living in a fantasy world, one that's not real. We withdraw into ourselves and block out everything else. It's like looking out a large picture window. We only see all the bad things that are going on, the killings, beatings, the rapes. So what we do is we get a real thick heavy blanket, and cover up our window in life. Trouble is, when you do that, you also block out all the good in life, like the birds, trees, the flowers, and also the sunshine. We live in a world of darkness.

The longer you live like that, the thicker your wall of rock becomes. Some people live their whole life that way. The ones, who get tired of living that way, must do what we are doing now, chip away at the rock, and chip away at our denial systems, one day at a time, one piece at time, until we reach it. Oh it's certainly not an easy road, it's a long journey, and often times a painful one. We often become afraid to remove that heavy blanket of a curtain we've put up. But in the end, it's like finding that pipestone that is buried underneath all this rock, penetrating our denial systems and finding our true selves. And once you do that, nobody can ever take that away from you, ever again.

Joe

Wow, I never thought of it that way.

Joe places the chisel on the last big piece of rock and the Elder lifts up the sludge hammer and delivers a last hard blow to the chisel and a the rock cracks causing a large chunk of the rock to fall. They both look on the ground to see that the red pipestone has finally been exposed. Joe jumps in excitement.

Joe

See that, yeah, yahoo, we've done it, I feel so good, I could cry.

Joe then takes a crow bar and shoves it underneath the flat sheet of red rock and tries to lift it up.

Elder

Be careful Joe, don't get too excited, be patient, you lift the pipestone to quickly, it will split into tiny sheets, then all our work will have been for nothing and we'll have to start all over again.

The slab of red rock breaks off into a perfect chunk. Joe lifts the slab over his head.

Joe

Thank you God, thank you creator. Thank you grandmothers and grandfathers. I thank you for this good life. To me this red rock is worth more than all the wealth in the world. Today, I begin my life all over again. Never again will I walk Mother Earth in shame, I will stand proud and tall and most of all, the thought of suicide will never ever be an option for me again. For the first time in my life, I feel connected to something greater than myself. My existence will no longer depend on what others think of me, but from only what I think of myself. Now I truly know where I belong and I take my place on Mother Earth with a sense of pride and dignity. My blood was spilled here to flow with the blood of my ancestors, to ground and connect me to my past, where I've been and where I've come from, to my present, where I am now, and to my future, where I am going, where I need to be. I will no longer walk a road that leads nowhere, for I have found my center, my balance in life. In this rock, I've found my spirit, my purpose, and my true self. I claim Mother Earth and my right to be here, the right for my people to be here, to once again teach my people to live in harmony with each other and all living things. To care for Mother Earth and learn all I can in order to become wise. For I am, "Black Eagle Thunderbird Man".

ABOUT TO AUTHOR

My name is Christopher Beach and I presently in Winnipeg Manitoba. I am a teacher and a counselor and have been teaching since I received my teaching degree from the University of Manitoba in 1991. I also have a counseling certificate from the same University.

I come from a large family of 11 children, 6 girls and 5 boys. 8 of my siblings have university degrees from the University of Manitoba and 3 of my sisters have their masters degree in Education field.

I have a total of 7 children and many other foster children which I raised mostly as a single parent.

For most of my career, I have worked with Aboriginal youth and believe I have a good understanding of their issues.

I am also of Aboriginal decent and am recognized as a Metis person, although I am eligible to be recognized by the Canadian government as a registered Indian.

I follow the Aboriginal culture and also conduct some of the teachings and ceremonies.

Through out my life, I have had many friends and relatives take their own lives and when one of my foster son committed suicide in 2005, I decided to write this book in order to help this epidemic that pledges our communities. Although I wrote this book for an Aboriginal youth audience, I believe anyone who reads this book will benefit from it.